Contents

MAILBOX MUFFINS

and
OTHER
RECIPES
from the
GULF COAST
HOMELESS

The Homeless of Oregon Place Apartments

J.P.
Keep homeless
in mind, for they
need all of our
help.

CHANGING LIVES PRESS

Changing Lives Press
www.changinglivespress.com

To purchase our books, please visit our website at www.continentalsalesinc.com
or contact Terry Wybel, Continental Sales, Inc., at wybelt@wybel.com or call 1-847-381-6530

Our titles are focused on books that impact peoples lives.
The authors we choose are those who have influenced or changed
the way we think, act, or process ideas and information.

EDITOR: Shari Johnson

COVER, TYPESETTING, AND BOOK DESIGN: Gary A. Rosenberg

ISBN-13: 978-0-9843047-4-5 • ISBN-10: 0-9843047-4-6

Printed in the United States of America

10   9   8   7   6   5   4   3   2   1

To all of you across the nation
who work to make the lives
of the homeless a bit easier
by providing food, shelter,
counseling, emotional support
and a listening ear, we thank
you. For the sacrificial giving
of your time and resources, we
thank you. For your dedication
to the homeless—we thank you.

FOREWORD

Marsha Barbour
First Lady of Mississippi

The first days after Hurricane Katrina hit are etched into my memory forever. Prior to August 29, 2005, I had never in my life witnessed so clearly the tremendous power of nature's wrath—homes gutted to empty shells, photographs trampled into the muddy ground, majestic live oaks stripped of their leaves. But what I will always remember most from those first moments following Katrina's fury is the unwavering courage and selflessness of our people.

I observed this same spirit of selflessness and community in the countless number of volunteers who began helping shortly after Katrina struck our Gulf Coast. Even locals—many of whom had lost just about everything they owned—were more concerned with assisting their neighbors or with helping the elderly couple down the road they did not want overlooked. Despite the gravity of the situation, people remained steadfast in their efforts to care for one another. Looking back, I know it was this unbelievable spirit that fueled me over those difficult first days and over the following months to do anything and everything I could to help our people.

For me and so many others, August 29, 2005, is a day that will forever hold life-changing memories. One of my most gut-wrenching recollections is flying over the Coast in a helicopter and seeing people wave their hands because they needed to be rescued. The thing that was most scary for me, however, was that I did not want to tell Haley how bad the situation really was. I was afraid he would have wanted me to come home . . . but I was there as Marsha Barbour, not as the First Lady of Mississippi.

On the ground, I was absolutely astounded by how much it meant for our people to have me and all the volunteers there speak with them, cry with them, and hope with them. Left with literally nothing but the clothes on their backs, they wanted and needed someone there for comfort, assurance and encouragement. That's why the overwhelming presence of faith-based organizations and the in-state and out-of-state volunteer groups played such an important part in the days and weeks after Katrina. These volunteers gave not only clothes and food to the hurricane victims, but also gave the most important thing of all—*hope*. I am so thankful for all the many people who helped our displaced residents, who listened to their problems, who lent a shoulder to cry on when times were tough. During the past year, I have realized time and time again what a crucial role these volunteers played in the aftermath of Katrina.

In retrospect, I've found that it's truly amazing when you are pulled from your comfort zone, how the important things in life become so apparent. And what mattered after Hurricane Katrina was being there for the people. That was most important to me—and to them. The selfless response of our citizens reminds me of a quote of Emerson's: "What lies behind us and what lies before us are tiny matters compared to what lies within us." This storm brought out the best in our people, and that Mississippi spirit makes Haley and me proud to serve.

Being on the Coast after Katrina was an experience that I will hold in my heart forever, and I truly feel that I got back more than I ever gave. My unending gratitude goes to all who have helped our people and our great state recover—in large and small ways. And most importantly, I am grateful to our people on the Coast who have put things into perspective for me—for showing me a greater way to live—a greater way to love.

The Coast continues to recover, and projects like Oregon Place are giving people a chance to remake their lives and take a step toward a brighter future. This book of recipes will benefit the mission of Oregon Place and help its residents.

Thank you for your help.

Marsha Barbour, First Lady of Mississippi

INTRODUCTION

William Richardson

They were so nearly invisible that I almost did not see them. I drove right by the small family of four gathered on the far side of a shopping center parking lot. It was late in the day, one that had been very stressful, and I was headed home for a family birthday dinner. Later I wondered how many times I had not seen people gathered in odd places with that certain look of hopelessness on their faces. Little did I know that over the next several years the briefly observed image of this family would haunt me as I started down a new, uncharted path to not only find homes for the homeless, but to find ways to restore their souls with pride, dignity, and hope.

In September of 2005, following Hurricane Katrina, I was asked by Mississippi Governor Haley Barbour to spearhead the creation of the Mississippi Hurricane Recovery Fund with the mission to raise "non-governmental," private sector monies to match federal funds in assisting the thousands of people who had lost so much in the hurricane. For the next three years my volunteer job as CEO was to serve as a full time fund raiser and assist with the recovery effort. Coming from the private sector, I had never been exposed to the "work" of the non-profit world. I was afforded the opportunity of meeting and working closely with some of the most resilient and determined people I have ever met. Volunteers from all ages, ethnic groups, and economic strata joined in the recovery process. Over one million volunteers from around the world came to work with hundreds of non-profits.

In my new position, I met two people who would shape my future. The first, Gulfport attorney Rodger Wilder, had taken a sabbatical from his law practice to serve as president of the Gulf Coast Community Foundation. Rodger and I are the same age, graduated from the same university, and had many common friends and interests, but we had never crossed paths. Rodger, a practicing attorney with an engineering degree, continues to provide the leadership and knowledge needed to create a stronger Gulf coast. Rodger and the Gulf Coast Community Foundation agreed to become administrator of the Fund's $32 million. It was through this work that we became great friends.

The second person's profile clearly did not fit with mine. Ellen Ratner, a New York liberal, is unlike anyone I have ever known. She is a ball of kinetic energy wrapped around a loving heart full of compassion for anyone in need. Additionally, Ellen is a salesperson driven by her passion to serve others.

In the early days following Katrina, Ellen, along with her partner, Cholene Espinoza, and new friend, Gulfport attorney Shantrell Nicks whom Ellen met on a plane five days after Katrina, became engaged in the relief and recovery efforts. Ellen and Cholene established a non-profit to serve the educational, recreational, and social needs of a rural community that had been trampled by the hurricane. They needed money (a place where Ellen seems to stay!) to develop the goals of their new entity. I met Ellen in July of 2006 when she learned that our Fund had "her" money that was needed for a new resource community center. We connected in spite of being total opposites and have had great fun in our continuing projects. And what insight she had—we did have her money.

Ellen and I were having so much fun working together on new projects that when Rodger stepped down from his active role with the Foundation, we recruited him to join us. His local knowledge, position in the community, legal skills, and eagerness to serve made him the ideal team member.

During the waning days of the Fund, some of my new friends from the coast's non-profit world asked me to help develop a business plan for a homeless shelter to replace one destroyed by Hurricane Katrina. Although I was new to the concept of supporting the homeless, I had developed business plans professionally for years. Besides, I could not find a good excuse to avoid helping my new friends who had supported me in the Recovery Fund's efforts.

When the non-profit I was helping determined that they did not want to go forward with their shelter plans, my role as supporter and advisor quickly turned into financial packager and developer. I had managed to find funding for the construction of a new shelter and did not want to let that money go unused. The need for homeless living accommodations was ever-growing.

In the months between signing on as an advisor to the day that I made it my personal goal to provide safe, secure, and comfortable living units for people that, but for the grace of God could be me, I called on my two friends Ellen and Rodger to become co-conspirators in this process. Ellen, a former mental health professional and president of Mississippi Cares International, Inc., quickly became a fountain of resources. Rodger, now a board member, just came along for the adventure—or so he would have us believe. We all agreed to create a national model for homeless advancement. We wanted to create an environment where people could live safely while receiving assistance and career training that would enable them to reenter the workforce with pride and dignity.

Mississippi Cares International, Inc., a not for profit Mississippi-chartered entity, accepted the role of sponsor for the project—clearly a leap of faith. We determined to become a facilitator by providing the capital and management skills to make housing a reality. Our plan included involving the local non-profits, who historically provide services to homeless, with the opportunity to serve as "lease agents" and case managers. Our goal proved to be more difficult than anticipated.

For over two years we struggled with county and city governments to find a location suitable for the project. This long struggle almost whipped us until the idea of purchasing an existing apartment unit to avoid the zoning issues materialized. Mississippi Cares International, Inc. purchased a Fannie Mae-owned 56-unit apartment complex in central Gulfport, Mississippi. Oregon Place apartments became our site for the homeless housing project.

Funds for this purchase came from two sources. One, Mississippi Development Authority's Disaster Recovery program's use of the U. S. Department of Housing and Urban Development Katrina Community Development Block Grant, a special fund established following Hurricane

Katrina to aid in the recovery of Transitional Workforce Housing on the Mississippi Gulf Coast; and two, the Gulf Coast Community Fund's Mississippi Hurricane Recovery Fund, which provided additional matching funds. These monies were used to purchase, restore, and furnish each unit—from chairs and beds, to knives, forks and spoons.

Our plan to provide a model for relocating homeless people from the woods (yes, I mean the woods) directly into air conditioned, two-bedroom apartments worked. This method has been termed as "street to home" by various national efforts. We have had success, sprinkled with a few failures. During the first six months, through solid case management provided by the non-profit organizations using our resource, some tenants have earned a GED (General Educational Development) and are now enrolled in college. Other tenants have mastered the basic skills of reading and writing, while some, on a more traditional path, have selected training or re-training to build new careers that offer hope for the future and an improvement in their economic conditions. Admittedly, a few tenants have elected to return to the woods to escape the stress of recovery.

While Ellen, Rodger and I have observed these transitions, our curiosities have gotten the best of us. How does this population survive in the woods? What trials do they overcome? Where do they get their food and how is it cooked without electricity or gas? Eating is very important to me! Ellen and Rodger wear their meals better than I do, but they, too, are good eaters. While sharing our project with a couple in Portland, Oregon, national talk radio host Lars Larson and his wife, Tina, one of the residents talked about the art of making mailbox muffins. This was too good to go unnoticed. Thus, we are proud to share with you recipes from the woods along with a few of the background stories told to us by the survivors who are now residents of Oregon Place.

My hope is that as you read about their lives and these interesting methods of cooking you will see the "nearly invisible people" that I did not; that you will open your hearts to extend a helping hand to those who need a hand up; and that you will count your blessings.

William Richardson

Lessons Learned from the Homeless

Don Sally

I grew up in Winnetka, Illinois, a prestigious suburb of Chicago. Not many worries about homelessness there. I left Winnetka after high school to live and work in California. One of my first jobs was in the laundry room of the San Diego Hilton. Later that year I moved to Santa Barbara and worked at a beachside hotel doing everything—cooking, solving guestroom issues, working the desk, night audit and more. I have several stories about the homeless from working at this beachside hotel. One of the more memorable was the frequent requests by my General Manager to drain and clean the Jacuzzi on the outdoor pool deck. Late at night, several homeless people would pitch in and get a few small boxes of tide from the coin laundry for 25 cents each. They would then have a big bubble bath party in the Jacuzzi and wash all their clothes—talk about ring around the tub! After all, it was Santa Barbara—they had to be clean and look good or they would be harassed and run out of town. Not much tolerance or understanding of the issues facing the homeless in that wealthy beachside paradise.

I have been drawn to food and serving people since I was very young—from the farming and supply-chain end to the tastes and combinations of ingredients and how they complement and interact with each other. I find this fascinating. My family owns and operates a big farm in Southern Illinois. Serving others has been instrumental in my success in the hospitality business. I work when others celebrate and play.

> They would then have a big bubble bath party in the Jacuzzi and wash all their clothes —talk about ring around the tub!

As a child, one of my earliest Christmas wishes was for an Easy Bake Oven. After graduating from culinary school 15 years later and then moving on to obtain my bachelor's degree in hospitality administration from the University of Nevada Las Vegas, I accepted a job working for Hyatt Resorts Hawaii. I had the opportunity to work in and help open some of the most prestigious resorts in the world at that time. After six years in Hawaii, I came to Mississippi to open the Silver Star Resort and Casino in Philadelphia, Mississippi. This was a very busy and successful operation from day one. We served more that 1.2 million meals per year and provided outstanding culinary excellence and equally good service and execution. This business requires flexibility and frequent moves. In Mississippi since 1994, I have opened seven casinos and resorts from the ground up and worked at numerous large and very successful casinos.

In the middle of 2010, I became fascinated with several projects that my friend and mentor, William Richardson, had been instrumental in developing on the Gulf Coast of Mississippi. This is what brought me to Oregon Place. The rest, as they say, is history. These people have touched my life. Their stories, the hardships they've endured, their weathered faces, their desperate yet kind eyes, and their smiles of appreciation are really quite amazing.

The ingenuity of the homeless when it comes to preparing food amazes me. Cans are not discarded. After using them for the purpose intended, they become cooking vessels, dishware, muffin tins, or anything else to fill a need. They also cook on foil and a variety of other items they can find that proves useful and reusable.

The inspiration for this book came from the mailbox oven, an innovation of Bobby Kelly's, who lived in the 28th Street Woods. He had been given a stainless steel mailbox by a steel fabricator after hurricane Katrina. The client who ordered it never picked it up, and it sat in the warehouse unclaimed for over two years. Bobby planned to sell it for scrap steel, but realized it could be used for something much more important.

The mailbox already had hooks installed on the top to hang it from a post or pole. Bobby pounded a pipe into the ground in close proximity to the fire pit, then found an L-shaped pipe of a smaller diameter that would fit into the first pipe. The completed pipe was five feet high and

As a child, one of my earliest Christmas wishes was for an Easy Bake Oven.

The inspiration for this book came from the mailbox oven, an innovation of Bobby Kelly's, who lived in the 28th Street woods.

extended about four feet over the fire pit. Adjustable chains were used to secure the mailbox to the pipe, allowing for heat regulation. The L-shaped pipe could swivel either over or away from the fire, regulating the heat in the oven even more. It also facilitated the loading and unloading of the food. Sticks, hangers, pipes and rags were used to move items in and out of the oven.

Not all of the recipes in this book are from the "homeless" days; some are family recipes, some are favorites from childhood and some are from working in hotels and restaurants prior to Katrina. The apartments at Oregon Place have "real" kitchens, so although the challenge isn't there any more, the food is just as good and satisfying!

One thing I have learned while working closely with these wonderful people is that no one is that far removed from this reality—a few simple twists of fate, some bad decisions and this could happen to any of us. Be thankful for a close family, friends and your health—there is a common thread that runs through most of these amazing stories involving those three elements.

I hope you will enjoy reading about a *slice* of their life and of the support this and other programs provide to help eliminate homelessness. After you have finished reading, please consider the following recipe:

> Be thankful for a close family, friends and your health— there is a common thread that runs through most of these amazing stories involving those three elements.

CASEROLE FOR THE HOMELESS

INGREDIENTS

- A dash of sympathy
- A sprinkling of understanding
- A generous helping of support and guidance
- Sprinkle with compassion
- Garnish with genuine concern

Mix the above ingredients with the right attitude and a desire to move forward. Add a good support system and some training, and you cannot fail. We have had wonderful success with this recipe here at Oregon Place. Try it—I think you'll like it.

Bon Appetite, Don Sally

Jobless to Homeless

Bobby Kelly

One's first impression of Bobby Kelly would probably be wrong. He's big, bald and tattooed—tattoos he got while incarcerated. Unfortunately, some people can't get past appearances and their own perceptions. In the case of Bobby Kelly, it would be their loss.

Bobby is a 53-year-old man who is working with a tutor, trying to get his GED (General Educational Development for high school equivalency diploma). He didn't finish high school for several reasons. In his words, "I really didn't learn anything. It wasn't due to my problems. It was due to other people's problems. Then I became the problem. You get tired of being pushed around. I was a poor kid—I mean dirt poor. I never had teachers that would actually take an interest in my reading and spelling. Now they call it [Attention Deficit Disorder, dyslexia]. In the seventies there was no such thing, I don't guess. I couldn't understand the words they were trying to teach me. They were always telling me that I wasn't trying hard, and I guess I did come to the point where I turned into, like, a violent kid or whatever. I didn't want to hear it anymore.

"I wound up in *Juvenile*. I don't really blame the school and the teachers—well, in a way I do and in a way I don't. Like I said, they never took any interest until I come to the point where I became the bully that they said I was. I done what they wanted me to do and I shouldn't have.

"But it's never too late to straighten up. I straightened up. I'm not gonna live up to what they want me to be. There's still people out there

You get tired of being pushed around. I was a poor kid—I mean dirt poor.

9

Bobby has worked hard from the time he was a kid making five dollars a day delivering milk.

today that say, 'Bobby, let's go,' and I say, 'No, man. You got me messed up. Go on out of my place!' I don't drink, I don't do drugs. I got one bad habit—I smoke cigarettes and I need to quit that. That's it."

Bobby has worked hard from the time he was a kid making five dollars a day delivering milk. At that time, the milk was in bottles and delivered to houses in wire baskets. Bobby's job was to run the baskets of milk behind the houses and leave them under boxes.

Since then he has done odd jobs such as carpentry and plumbing, but has mainly worked the Mississippi River, starting as a deckhand on boats pushing barges and moving up to tackleman on chemical barges. When asked if he had any technical training he said, "Most of it I hand-learned. I was thirteen years old when I started out. I worked on deck for fifteen years and I learned everything—there wasn't nothing to that. But I had to go through school for the tackleman's ticket. I don't know how I did that, but I passed the test. It took me about two years of studying to get to that test."

So how does a hard worker like Bobby Kelly wind up homeless for the past eight years? "Eyesight. I was doing fence work and it got where I couldn't tie the ties to the fences anymore, and I was messing them up real bad. I was trying to fake it, but I got fired. I don't blame the guy, because that's his business. The ties needed to be done right. I did some part-time jobs here and there. I worked for CRS Roofing, but my eyes were so bad I fell off the roof and they had to let me go. I don't blame them, though. John at CRS Roofing knew my eyes were bad and he gave me part-time work mowing his lawn

So how does a hard worker like Bobby Kelly wind up homeless for the past eight years?

"Come to find out, it was cataracts. I had the cataracts of a ninety-year-old man at the time and I just gradually lost my sight. My right eye went out first, then my left eye was right behind it. Everything was shadows for about two and a half years. I sat in the woods during that time and Jennifer [Bobby's girlfriend] took care of everything. She talked me into calling my sister, so I did and we started going to the Gulf Coast Family Clinic to get my eyes fixed. It ended up that the Lion's club paid for my cataract surgery. Now I just have to have reading glasses, but as far as seeing goes, I'm good."

Before Bobby lost his job he was renting a little trailer from his sister.

When he could no longer pay rent, he and Jennifer lived on the streets for about a week or so. He figured that they needed to get somewhere so they wouldn't be harassed, so they went from the streets to a cardboard box that he covered with plastic, then to a tent. "My first tent got flooded out so bad that I said it would never happen again. So we hustled parts. I put up corner poles and then got a tent from Ms. Chris and Eddie at Gulf Coast Community Mission. They gave out tents and stuff like that."

When asked about his thoughts at that time—whether he was upset about his situation, if he struggled with wondering how he ended up there—he said, "You really couldn't worry about all that 'cause you had to fight the elements of the day. You had to get out there. You had to hustle groceries, you had to hustle cans. We walked the streets picking up cans to make a few dollars here and there for different things Jennifer needed. Worry never did actually come in until you laid down. Then you was thinking, 'Well, I got to do this tomorrow. You have to start the whole process again tomorrow.' But I never did dwell on it. Never did. I always said, 'Maybe six months and we'll be out of this situation.' Next thing I know it's eight and a half years later."

About cooking, Bobby said, "I had what we call a burn pit. I dug a hole in the ground because I didn't do like the other people did—that caused a lot of trouble with the police and the fire department. I had tin around mine. I used the bottom of a big barbeque pit—pretty good size. I set it in the ground and had a grill over it. We hustled everyday for a scrap of whatever we could use. If there was a piece of string three inches long we would pick it up and take it with us because one day we would have to use it to tie something with it. We used everything."

Bobby said that they found the utensils they used for cooking and made do with most everything else—like using tin cans to cook in. About 98% of the food came from food pantries and local homeless feeding centers.

Concerning the food, Bobby says, "You get cheese, flour and lots of peanut butter. You get meat, maybe a couple of chicken breasts or thighs, packs of hot dogs, tuna fish, crackers, grease, cooking oils, Vienna sausages, SPAM, baking mixes and stuff like that. The muffins you can just mix with water. You don't need no eggs or milk or none of that. You

> We walked the streets picking up cans to make a few dollars here and there for different things we needed. Worry never did actually come in until you laid down.

got to remember that we were living in the woods and in the summer-time, none of that stuff is going to keep. You have to use it immediately. Wintertime is a little different. You could hold it a little bit longer, depending on the weather.

"You can eat pretty good as long as you know where to go and how to do it—and you have to know how to talk to the people. But one time me and Jennifer lived on bananas for about a week. I can't remember what that was all about. It might have been when my eyes got so bad I couldn't get out no more. We could actually go to the food pantry once a month. You don't get much because they have a lot of people. But you appreciate it."

Bobby was asked if he ever had to go out on the street and beg. "No, and I will never do that. It hurt me just going to the church and asking for [food]."

Bobby was living in the 28th Street woods when Hurricane Katrina hit. "We didn't know the hurricane was coming. We didn't have any communication out there at that time. We had no portable battery radios or anything like that. We just saw people scrambling on the streets and stuff, but we never paid any attention. We had had a couple of the storms years before that didn't do anything, so we really didn't pay any attention and didn't think about any shelters or anything. We rode it out. We didn't stay in the tent. Every now and then we would go clear off the debris. But actually, in that part of the woods in Gulfport where I was staying, my tent is still standing after Hurricane Katrina. I'll tell you something else—I went back and checked the spot where we had lived in the cardboard box. I just had to know. Everything else was wiped out, but that cardboard box and that plastic was still standing. I couldn't believe it."

Was Bobby scared during the hurricane? "Yeah. I was scared. We had trees snapping all around us and wind blowing. We would fight our way up to the road. There was a house on the corner and we went and sat on his porch for a while, and then would fight our way back to the woods to check on our tent because that's all the belongings we had. Yeah, it was scary."

After Katrina, they got water and MREs (Meal, Ready-to-Eat) from the military. "I never did get nothing from FEMA (Federal Emergency

"You can eat pretty good as long as you know where to go and how to do it—and you have to know how to talk to the people."

"We didn't know the hurricane was coming. We didn't have any communication out there at that time.

Management Agency). They said you could get three-hundred and fifty dollars for clothes. We didn't get nothing. We didn't take nothing from them, but we didn't lose nothing. We got water, ice, stuff like that." Bobby and Jennifer stayed in the same little area of the woods for another five years.

Now Bobby lives at Oregon Place. He would like people to know that he's a good person, and that he would love to get back to work—have a steady job. He would like to go to work on the boats again, but Jennifer suffers from schizophrenia and he feels that he can't leave her. Someone has to be with her because of the medication she takes. He would also like to write a book one day—he certainly has an interesting story to tell. "But I've got a lot more education to get together before I do that."

He would also like to write a book one day—he certainly has an interesting story to tell.

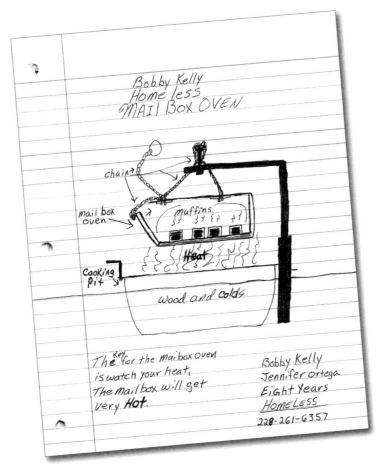

Bobby Kelly
Home less
MAIl Box OVEN

chain?

mail box oven

muffins

Heat

Cooking Pit

wood and colds

The key for the mailbox oven is watch your heat, The mailbox will get very **Hot.**

Bobby Kelly
Jennifer Ortega
Eight Years
HOMELESS
228-261-6357

RECIPES FROM THE 28TH STREET WOODS

Bobby Kelley is the innovator of the mailbox oven. Following are some of the recipes he created while living in the woods.

MAILBOX CORNBREAD

INGREDIENTS

1 box of cornbread mix (any brand)

Water (according to directions on box)

YOU WILL ALSO NEED:

Empty 1-inch deep tuna fish cans

Cornbread makes any meal even better. It also helps stretch the food further.

Heat mailbox oven. Combine cornbread mix and water and mix well. Fill tuna fish cans with mixture and bake for 45 minutes. Remove mailbox from fire and allow to cool. Eat cornbread straight from cans.

HOT, BAKED PINK SALMON CAKES

INGREDIENTS

2 cans of pink salmon

1 diced onion

1 can of diced carrots

$\frac{1}{2}$ cup biscuit baking mix

3 tablespoons hot sauce

1 tablespoon red pepper

1 tablespoon black pepper

Omega-3 nutrition and tasty, too!

Heat mailbox oven. Mix all ingredients together. Distribute mixture into empty salmon cans. Put inside mailbox oven and let cook for 30 minutes. Remove cans from mailbox oven and let cool. Enjoy. Serves two.

MAILBOX MUFFINS

Our signature recipe!

Heat mailbox oven over wood coals. Mix all ingredients in large, empty can. Distribute batter evenly into tuna fish cans and place in hot mailbox oven. Bake for 30–40 minutes. (Check muffins at 30 minutes to see if they are done). Remove mailbox oven from fire and let cool. When completely cool, remove muffins from mailbox oven and enjoy eating the muffins right out of the cans. You can also top muffins with peanut butter, jelly, or both. Serves four.

INGREDIENTS

1 box muffin mix
(any brand or flavor)

1 egg

Water (amount according to muffin mix instructions)

YOU WILL ALSO NEED:

Mailbox oven

1 large empty can for mixing ingredients

4 empty, clean, 1-inch deep tuna fish cans for baking muffins

MAILBOX-BAKED BARBEQUE CHICKEN

Finger lickin' good! Got a crowd? Just add more chicken.

Heat mailbox over wood coals. Wash and dry leg quarters and season with salt, black pepper, garlic salt, and hot sauce. Wrap leg quarters in aluminum foil and place in heated mailbox oven. Let bake over coals 2 to $2^1/_2$ hours. Remove leg quarters from mailbox oven. Cover with barbeque sauce and enjoy.

Conventional oven: Bake at 350 degrees for approximately one hour.

INGREDIENTS

2 chicken leg quarters

$^1/_4$ teaspoon salt

$^1/_4$ teaspoon black pepper

$^1/_2$ teaspoon garlic salt

1 teaspoon hot sauce

Barbeque sauce

YOU WILL ALSO NEED:

Aluminum foil

INGREDIENTS

4 sliced rings of canned pineapple

Brown sugar

Yellow or white cake mix
(any brand)

1 egg

$1/_2$ tablespoon butter

Water (according to recipe
on cake mix box)

Cooking oil

YOU WILL ALSO NEED:

4 empty 4-inch-deep cans

MAILBOX OVEN PINEAPPLE UPSIDE-DOWN CAKE

So good, makes you want to slap yo' mama!

Heat mailbox oven over wood coals. Oil the empty 4-inch cans well with cooking oil. Combine cake mix, egg, water, and butter. Mix well. Put 1 slice of pineapple into each can. Spoon $1/_2$ tablespoon of brown sugar over pineapple ring, followed by cake batter. Put cans into mailbox oven and bake for 30 minutes. Remove mailbox oven from hot coals and allow to cool. Remove cans from mailbox oven and turn them upside down to remove cake. Enjoy. Serves four.

INGREDIENTS

1 can of chunk chicken

$1/_2$ cup diced onion

$1/_4$ teaspoon black or red pepper

$1/_2$ cup biscuit mix

MAILBOX OVEN-BAKED HOT CHICKEN PIE

Cans are multifunctional when cooking in the woods. Once they have performed their original function, they are washed and used as baking pans or for dishware.

Heat mailbox oven. Mix all ingredients together. Pour into empty cans. Bake for about 40 minutes. Allow mailbox oven to cool, then remove cans. Can be topped with warm cream of mushroom soup. Enjoy. Serves four (small cans) or two (larger cans).

CHUNKED TURKEY AND RICE

"Cooking over an open-fire wood pit takes longer time than usual. The cooking time for this dish is between one and two hours."

Boil rice in a pot till half done. Mix in onion, hot sauce, and tomato sauce. Continue cooking for 1 hour. Add can of turkey. Serves four.

Stovetop: Will take about 30–40 minutes cooking time.

INGREDIENTS

1 12-ounce can chunk turkey

1 onion, diced

1 teaspoon hot sauce

1 can of tomato sauce

1 cup rice

2 cups water

MAILBOX OVEN-BAKED TUNA, GREEN BEAN, MACARONI & CHEESE CASSEROLE

Easily converts to "kitchen" cooking.

Heat mailbox oven. Cook macaroni and drain. Add cheese sauce packs, tuna, green beans and onion to macaroni and dish into empty ham cans. Cook in mailbox oven for 20 minutes. Remove mailbox oven from heat. Enjoy dish straight from ham cans. Serves two or four, depending on appetites.

Conventional oven: Put ingredients in casserole dish and bake at 350 degrees for 30 minutes.

INGREDIENTS

2 cans of tuna fish

2 cans of green beans

2 boxes of macaroni and cheese

1 diced onion

YOU WILL ALSO NEED:

2 empty ham cans

CHICKEN JAMBALAYA

*Canned goods keep well in the woods
and they are easy to come by.*

Cook rice in a pot till half done over an open-fire wood pit. Add the rest of the ingredients and continue cooking for 45 minutes. Allow to cool. Enjoy! Feeds four (more or less).

INGREDIENTS

2 cans of chicken

1 onion, diced

2 tablespoons red pepper

1 cup of rice

1 can cut green beans

1 can whole kernel corn

3 tablespoons hot sauce

$1/_2$ tablespoon salt

$1 1/_2$ cup water

COLD, RAINY DAY RAMEN NOODLE CASSEROLE

*If the weather is too miserable to be outside,
the "candles cooker" is another ingenious idea.
It consists of a can with several candles in it.
The food is placed in another can or receptacle and
placed on top of the candles cooker. About this recipe
Bobby says, "It really warms you up on a cold day!"*

Cook ramen noodles according to package directions using a candles cooker. Drain noodles, then add the remaining ingredients. Mix well and enjoy. Serves two to three.

INGREDIENTS

2 packages of ramen noodles

1 can of sweet peas

$1/_2$ onion, diced

3 tablespoons mayonnaise

1 tablespoon black pepper

2 tablespoons hot sauce

TUNA BAKE— MAILBOX OVEN CAKES

Tuna is inexpensive to buy or is usually available at the food pantries.

Heat mailbox oven first. Use tuna can to cook in. Mix eggs, onion, tuna fish, red pepper, salt, and black pepper. Put in 3-inch, oiled cooking cans and put in hot mailbox oven. Don't put mailbox oven back over the fire. Cook about 30 or 40 minutes. It will cook slowly.

INGREDIENTS

3 eggs, beaten

1 large (3"x 2") can tuna fish

$1/2$ onion, diced

$1/2$ teaspoon red pepper

$1/8$ teaspoon salt

$1/4$ teaspoon black pepper

Also needed:

2–3 empty tuna cans for baking and serving

COLD, RAINY DAY SOUP

Not only will you get your veggies, but "It will warm you up. Yum, Yum, Yum!"

Put all ingredients in a pot and stir. Put pot on candle cooker. This recipe should take about 45 minutes on a candle cooker. Serves three to four.

For the kitchen: You can either use a crockpot and cook slowly, or cook in saucepan on top of stove for 20–30 minutes.

INGREDIENTS

1 can mixed vegetables

1 can sliced carrots

1 can sweet corn

1 can tomato sauce

2 cans (3" x 2") tuna fish

$1/2$ onion, diced

$1/2$ teaspoon red pepper

2 teaspoons hot sauce

2 teaspoons black pepper

MORE RECIPES FROM BOBBY

Not made in the woods, but just as good!

INGREDIENTS

2 whole cabbages, shredded

2 cups mayonnaise

1 cup carrots, shredded

1 tablespoon celery salt

2 tablespoons sugar

2 tablespoons vinegar

1 cup red onion, chopped

$1^{1}/_{2}$ cup mixed raisins

COLE SLAW WITH DRESSING

Barbecues just aren't complete without coleslaw!

Mix all ingredients in bowl. Chill for a couple of hours and serve cold. Serves several people.

INGREDIENTS

1 package spaghetti noodles

1 can (or jar) spaghetti sauce

1 pound cooked ground beef

1 pound Velveeta® Cheese

SIMPLY BAKED SPAGHETTI

*Quick and easy to prepare;
stick-to-the-ribs goodness!*

Boil noodles for about 7–10 minutes and drain. Grease baking pan and layer ingredients with a layer of cheese on top. Bake at 350 degrees for 30 minutes. Serves four.

Guilty by Association

Crystal Raley

Crystal Raley is a 34-year-old single woman who is an example of what can happen when life goes terribly wrong. "I never thought in a million years that I would be in this situation. I never looked down on anybody because of their situation. I always felt sorry for people. I couldn't understand how people got like this. And then it's me."

Raised by her mom in East Biloxi, Mississippi, Crystal, or "Crit," as her mother called her, feels that she had a stable home environment. Her mom worked in housekeeping at Keesler Air Force Base. She didn't drink or do drugs, but Crystal's dad was an alcoholic and her parents divorced when she was around eight years old. He was pretty much out of the picture while she was growing up. "He mostly wasn't such a good person. He spent a lot of time in prison for armed robbery and other illegal things." However, Crystal was able to have a relationship with him before he died, shortly before Hurricane Katrina. When asked if she had experienced any abuse when she was a child she said, "No, but everybody says I should have got a spanking now and then!"

Crystal quit school when she was in the tenth grade. "I just had problems with the other kids. I've always been shy and the nervous type. I cried every day at school." She worked at various jobs; for a while at Keesler Air Force base in housekeeping, then at the casinos as room service cashier and she "pretty much did the computer."

Then Katrina hit the Gulf Coast and everything changed for Crystal. She and her mother fled north to Vancleave, Mississippi, to stay with

> "I never thought in a million years that I would be in this situation. I couldn't understand how people got like this. And then it's me."

some friends. When they returned to Biloxi, they found that everything they had was destroyed. "We stayed in a shelter for a while and then I went to prison for three and a half years."

Crystal was in a car with a friend who had a small baggie of cocaine. It didn't matter that it wasn't hers, she went to prison for possession. She broke down when asked about the prison experience. "Horrible . . . I'm just not a crime person . . ."

The day she was released, two years ago, some of her mother's friends picked her up because her mom was very ill. About a month after that, her mom passed away. It was extremely hard for Crystal, as they were very close—she was all the family Crystal had left. It was at this point when Crystal became homeless.

"When I first got out [of prison], it was so hard—it's still hard—to get a job. A lot of people want to do a background check and if they see a felony on your record, they don't call you back. You get stuck. Each case is different. They don't give you a chance to explain. They just see a felony, or they have some questions for me, or some of the applications say, 'Have you ever been convicted of a felony?' If you're honest and you say yes, a felony could be killing your whole family or it could be . . . [like what happened to her], or like the time I was in the car with my mom and she had some Naprosyn or Naproxen or whatever it is called, but it was in the console and not in the bottle. When we got stopped, the cop wanted to arrest her, but then believed her—that it was a prescription."

Crystal's mom left her a house, but she couldn't get the certificate of occupancy because she couldn't get the money to pay all the deposits to get the utilities turned on, and now the taxes are falling behind. "I haven't lost the house yet, but I'm not allowed to be there. A judge banned me from the property until I get everything squared away. I have until August [2011], but I don't see it happening. They will sell it, and I won't get any money for it. The taxes are less than two thousand dollars. I'm worrying myself sick over it 'cause I see losing a whole house and everything in it. I'm looking everywhere for a job, and I don't know what to do anymore. But something is gonna happen. I'm gonna work it out."

When Crystal first got out of prison, she lived with Charlie. The two of them have been together on and off for eleven or twelve years.

"I got stuck in a rut, and it's hard as hell to crawl out of this hole."

"I would wander the streets and just not be able to sleep for like sometimes eight or nine days at a time . . . because I had nowhere to go. Nowhere.

"He's a good person. He treats me well—probably better than I treat him sometimes. If it wasn't for him, I'd be totally alone. But with the job situation and lack of money, things just started going downhill. I got stuck in a rut, and it's hard as hell to crawl out of this hole.

"Sometimes Charlie was helping his sister of whatever, and I wasn't used to being homeless and didn't know where to go or what to do, so I just kind of took off and tried it on my own. I would wander the streets and just not be able to sleep for like sometimes eight or nine days at a time—and not because of alcohol or drugs, but because I had nowhere to go. Nowhere. And it's horrible in the area where I was living in Biloxi.

"You can't stay in one place for long in public, and I just didn't know where to go. I just walked and walked and walked by myself. I noticed that a bunch of homeless people have different little groups. But I was totally by myself and didn't know where to go. I've been beaten and things were done to me because I was out there alone."

Someone Crystal thought was a nice guy and had been a good friend to both her and Charlie for years would see her in the street and say, "Crystal, I hate to see you out here like this. You don't have to be, you know. Come and take a shower, or if you need to lay down for a while you know you can come to my house."

Crystal had been to his house many times before this, but she didn't want to impose on anyone. Finally, she was so delirious from sleep deprivation she couldn't stand it anymore. She went to his house and said, "I think I'll take you up on that offer now." He went to his bedroom to sleep and Crystal slept in a chair in the living room. She woke to his dragging her to the floor by her hair, ". . . beating the hell out of me and ripping my clothes off. I was screaming and screaming, then the neighbor had to bust out the kitchen window to get in and get him off of me."

Crystal happened to hear about Oregon Place when she was at Safe Place and overheard someone talking about it. "I never thought I had a chance. I filled out an application and I actually got in."

Crystal was going to barber school when her life got off track. At the end of her interview, when she was asked about her dreams and ambitions, she said, "I want to go back to school and get my license to be a barber." Crystal Raley is back on track.

> "I've been beaten and things were done to me because I was out there alone."

> "I want to go back to school and get my license to be a barber."

COOKIN' WITH CRIT!

Crystal's recipes come from "Some things that we've made for people over the years."

VIETNAMESE DIPPING SAUCE

INGREDIENTS

$1/2$ cup fish sauce

$1/4$ cup sugar

$1/8$ cup crushed garlic

1 whole lemon, wedged and squeezed

3 diced cayenne peppers

There is a large community of Vietnamese people living in East Biloxi, and Crit is fond of Asian food.

Mix all ingredients together for dipping beef strips or pork.

Note: You can purchase fish sauce in the Asian section of your grocery store or at an Oriental food store.

VIETNAMESE PO-BOY

INGREDIENTS

1 6-inch Po-Boy bun

3 full-length slices of cucumber

$1/4$ carrot, shredded

2 sprigs of mint leaves

4 slices of duck, pork, or beef

Soy sauce

Forget watercress sandwiches—the mint leaves, cucumber and carrot make this Po-Boy refreshing and different.

Make a sandwich and top with (or dip in) soy sauce.

SALAD DRESSING

Tart and "fishy."

Mix well and serve over salad, baked potato, steamed veggies, etc.

INGREDIENTS

2 tablespoons fish sauce

$1/_8$ cup pickle juice

Dash of garlic powder

2 tablespoons mayonnaise

Sprinkle with black pepper

BEEF & BEANS

If you are craving something hot & spicy, this versatile recipe will do the trick. Serve it with a fork, wrap it in a flour tortilla for a burrito "to go," or make an all-time favorite—tacos.

Sauté first four ingredients. Serve with pinto beans and soft tortillas or fill taco shells with sautéed mixture.

INGREDIENTS

1 pound of cubed (small pieces) beef

1 large fresh jalapeno, chopped

2 tomatoes, diced

1 onion, diced

Pinto beans

Taco shells (optional)

CHEESY JALAPENO BREAD

Cornbread that bites you back!

Mix Jiffy as directed on box. Let sit for 30 minutes, then add all other ingredients. Bake 13–15 minutes or until golden. Serves four or more.

INGREDIENTS

1 package Jiffy® Cornbread Mix

1 can cream style corn

2 jalapenos, chopped

$1/_2$ cup shredded cheddar cheese

ASIAN STYLE SHRIMP & NOODLES

INGREDIENTS

15 medium shrimp, cleaned and peeled

1 large package Thai noodles

$1/2$ package bean spouts

$1/3$ onion, chopped

$1/2$ bell pepper, chopped

2 cloves garlic, chopped

Cayenne pepper

Soy sauce

Butter (enough to sauté shrimp and vegetables)

Naturally, fresh shrimp is abundant on the Coast, but don't let that stop you if you happen to be land-locked. Using pre-peeled, pre-cleaned, even pre-cooked shrimp won't hurt this recipe a bit.

Sauté onion, bell pepper, garlic, bean sprouts and shrimp in butter. Prepare noodles as directed on package, then drain. Add seasoning packet to noodles, then add noodles to sautéed ingredients and sprinkle with cayenne pepper and soy sauce. Serves four.

FRIED RICE

INGREDIENTS

2 cups cooked and cooled jasmine rice

2 scrambled eggs

1 cup cooked meat (pork, chicken, or shrimp)

$1/2$ cup cooked vegetables (preferably carrots)

3 cloves minced garlic

3–4 tablespoons oil

Create away and make this recipe your own. You get to choose the meat, the veggies— and with the exotic flavor of jasmine rice, the tang of garlic and the surprise of scrambled eggs, it's bound to be a hit.

In large non-stick skillet, heat oil then add all ingredients and stir-fry. Serves four.

MOM'S SPAM® & RICE DISH

"Poor Mom, she couldn't cook at all, but she made this and I liked it. After my parents divorced my dad would say, 'Is your mom still subjecting you to that SPAM and rice dish?' "

Combine all ingredients in pot and bring to a boil, then simmer about 30 minutes. Serves four.

INGREDIENTS

1 can SPAM, cubed

1 can tomatoes, diced

1 onion, chopped

1 bell pepper, chopped

1 cup uncooked rice

2 cups of water.

Salt and pepper to taste.

SAUSAGE SPAGHETTI

Need to give some pizazz to an old stand-by? The sausage and celery in this recipe give spaghetti a new look and taste.

Sauté sausage and onion. Mix first seven ingredients together in pot and simmer for 30 minutes. Serve over cooked spaghetti noodles. Serves four.

INGREDIENTS

3 whole smoked sausages (or one loop sausage), any flavor, diced or sliced

1 whole onion, diced

Dash of salt

Dash of pepper

$1^1/_2$ stalks of celery, chopped

1 tablespoon garlic, minced

1 jar of Ragu® Pasta Sauce

1 8-ounce package spaghetti, cooked

STUFFED SAUSAGE

*Something very different—
serve as a main course or as an appetizer.*

INGREDIENTS

4 large smoked sausages

$1/2$ onion, diced

$1/2$ cup cream cheese

2 jalapeno peppers, diced

Sauté onions. Cut sausages in half lengthwise and hollow out each half. Chop the scooped out meat and mix with onion, cheese and peppers. Put mixture back in the hollowed-out sausage halves and bake at 375 degrees for 25 minutes. Serves four.

CORNED BEEF SPECIAL

Good for St. Patrick's Day (or any day).

INGREDIENTS

1 6-ounce package noodles

1 can cream of chicken soup

$1/2$ cup evaporated milk

1 can corned beef

1 cup grated cheese

$1/3$ cup chopped onion

$1/2$ cup potato chips,
crumbled

Cook noodles and drain. Combine soup, milk, corned beef, cheese, onion, and noodles in baking dish and top with chips. Bake at 425 degrees for 15–20 minutes. Serves four.

TUNA NOODLE SALAD

Ramen noodles are versatile (can be boiled or eaten right out of the package), inexpensive, and are a common ingredient in many of the recipes.

Drain tuna. Crumble noodles and let them sit in water till limp. Drain noodles. Mix all ingredients together and serve. Makes three or four servings.

INGREDIENTS

1 large can tuna

2 packages of ramen noodles

6 packs mayonnaise (from the food bar at many places) or 6 tablespoons

Dash of black pepper

VEGETABLE CASSEROLE

A vegetarian's delight—or a nutritious meal when meat isn't available.

Mix all ingredients except crackers and pour into 13 x 9 inch baking dish. Top with cracker crumbs and bake at 350 degrees for 35 minutes. Serves two or three.

INGREDIENTS

2 cans mixed vegetables

1 can of corn

1 onion, chopped

1 cup mayonnaise

2 cups grated cheese

1 package cracker crumbs

1 stick of butter

CRIT'S HOMEMADE TOMATO SOUP

This delicious soup is easy to make—and a perfect way to utilize a bumper crop of tomatoes!

Cut up tomatoes and onion. Put all ingredients except cheese in a blender. After blended well, put into pot and simmer on stovetop for $1^1/_2$ hours. Grate cheese on top and serve with saltines.

Soup thickens while simmering. Makes approximately 3 cups.

INGREDIENTS

1 cup water

5 whole fresh tomatoes

$^1/_2$ onion

$^1/_2$ teaspoon garlic powder

$^1/_2$ teaspoon Italian seasoning

$^1/_8$ teaspoon black pepper

Grated cheese of choice

YOU WILL ALSO NEED

A blender

BIG B'S SHRIMP SALAD

Summer salad doesn't get any more refreshing than this. Dice the shrimp into small pieces or use pre-packaged small, salad shrimp and it's perfect to serve on crackers.

Combine all of the ingredients and chill. Serves three to four.

INGREDIENTS

1 pound shrimp, cleaned and boiled

3 stalks celery, diced

$^1/_2$ cup black olives, diced

1 cup cottage cheese

3 cloves garlic, crushed

Salt and pepper to taste

CRIT'S "WOW" CHOPS

Wow indeed!

Marinate chops in mixture of chili sauce and soy sauce overnight. Bake marinated pork chops for 30–40 minutes at 350 degrees. Cook rice according to package directions. Fry eggs over-easy. Top a bed of rice with one pork chop and one egg. Serves four.

INGREDIENTS

4 center-cut pork chops

$1/2$ cup chili sauce

$1/2$ cup soy sauce

1 cup jasmine rice

4 eggs

HEALTHY PRUNE CHICKEN

Looking for a new, delicious way to serve chicken?
This is it!

Sauté onion in mixture of oil, all-spice, pepper and garlic powder. Add chicken and cook 5 minutes on each side. Add orange juice and prunes, cover, and simmer for 10 minutes. Serves five.

INGREDIENTS

5 chicken breasts boned

1 tablespoon vegetable oil

$1/2$ cup onion, chopped

$3/4$ teaspoon all-spice

$3/4$ cup orange juice

Dash of pepper

Dash of garlic powder

$1/4$ cup of chopped prunes

CABBAGE RAVAGE

*If you haven't cooked with cabbage lately,
this is a good place to start.*

INGREDIENTS

1 head of cabbage, chopped

1 12-ounce can cream of
celery soup

1 12-ounce can beef broth

1 pound ground beef

$1/4$ cup minced onion

$1/2$ tablespoon garlic powder

$1/2$ bell pepper, chopped fine

Sauté ground beef and bell pepper with a dash of pepper for about 8–10 minutes. Drain excess fat. Boil cabbage in $2^1/_2$ cups of water over medium heat until tender, then drain. Combine cream of celery soup, beef broth, minced onions and garlic powder in a saucepan with ground beef mixture. Let simmer about 10 minutes, then pour over cabbage. Serve with JIFFY® mix cornbread. Serves four.

CRIT'S CREAMY SHRIMP

Not low-cal, but who cares?

INGREDIENTS

$1/4$ pound butter (1 stick)

1 onion, chopped

1 can cream style corn

1 can whole kernel corn

1 can potato soup

1 teaspoon liquid crab boil

$1/2$ quart half and half cream

$1/2$ pint whipping cream

$1^1/_2$ pound raw shrimp,
peeled and cleaned

Sauté onion in large pot with butter. Add all other ingredients and simmer for about an hour. Serves four or more.

STUFFED POTATOES

Add a salad and you've got a complete meal.

Bake potatoes until soft at 400 degrees for 45 minutes to one hour. Cut in half, lengthwise. Scoop flesh of potatoes into a bowl and cream with cream cheese, pimento cheese, chives, and bacon. Top with grated Mozzarella and bake for 10 minutes. Serves four (or two with big appetites).

INGREDIENTS

2 large baking potatoes

$3/4$ cup cream cheese

$1/2$ cup pimento cheese

$1/8$ cup chives

$1/2$ cup fried bacon, crispy

Mozzarella cheese, grated

MUSHROOM TOAST

Got some bread that's a bit stale?
Try this clever recipe to put some life back into it.

Sauté mushrooms and onion in butter. Spread on bread and sprinkle with paprika and parmesan cheese. Bake at 300 degrees for about five minutes. Serves six, or cut in triangles or squares and serve as an appetizer.

INGREDIENTS

6 slices of bread

1 package fresh mushrooms, chopped

2 tablespoons butter

1 onion, minced

Paprika

Parmesan cheese, grated

CRIT'S DELICIOUS HAMBURGERS

A new twist on 'burgers, for sure!

Blend all ingredients in a bowl. Prepare burgers the size you prefer and grill or put in oven until done. Serves four or more.

INGREDIENTS

$1 1/2$ pounds ground beef

1 can chicken noodle soup

1 teaspoon minced garlic

$1/3$ onion, chopped

$1/2$ cup shredded cheese

1 egg

SPARKLING VIRGIN SUNRISE

Dee-lightful!

INGREDIENTS

1/2 glass soda water

1/2 glass sunny delight

3–4 drops grenadine

2 fresh cherries

Pour soda water in glass first, then orange juice, then grenadine. Top with cherries. Makes one glassful.

"SWEET" FRUIT SALAD

A colorful salad to dress up your table. Getting your fruit serving just doesn't get any better than this.

INGREDIENTS

1 kiwi, peeled

1 banana, peeled

15 grapes

10 strawberries

1/4 cup sweetened condensed milk

Cut up fruit into small pieces and put into bowl. Drizzle sweetened condensed milk on top. Serves two or three, depending on serving size. (That would be one serving for sweetened condensed milk lovers!)

NO-BAKE COOKIES

No-bake means no heat in the kitchen when the weather is hot.

INGREDIENTS

2 cups raw, old-fashioned oats

3/4 cup chunky peanut butter

1/3 bag miniature marshmallows

1/2 cup melted, semi-sweet chocolate

Mix all ingredients well. Mixture will be thick and pasty. Roll into balls. Place on parchment paper and pat flat. Let sit about 1 1/2–2 hours. They will get firm.

PUTTIN' ON THE RITZ

Another no-bake treat!

Spread peanut butter on 10 of the 20 crackers. Put the other 10 crackers on top. Place on waxed paper or cookie sheet. Pour melted chocolate over the peanut butter sandwiches. Let sit until chocolate hardens. Makes ten delicious "sandwiches."

INGREDIENTS

20 Ritz® Crackers

1 cup peanut butter

1 cup melted milk chocolate
(or dark chocolate if preferred)

SPICY PEANUT BUTTER MILK SHAKE

A shake that will shake you up.

Fill blender with ice cream. Add all other ingredients and blend until creamy. Makes a great shake. Two servings.

INGREDIENTS

Vanilla ice cream

4 tablespoons smooth peanut butter

$1/2$ teaspoon cayenne pepper

$1/3$ cup milk

BANANA SMOOTHIE

Perfect on a hot summer day!

Put everything in blender and mix well. Chill and enjoy. One serving.

INGREDIENTS

1 whole banana

$1/2$ cup evaporated milk

$1/2$ cup whole milk

2 packets of Sweet'N Low® artificial sweetener

4 ice cubes

CHERRY BANANA MUFFINS

INGREDIENTS

1/2 cup dried cherries

1 banana (mashed)

2 cups oats

1 egg

1 tablespoon cinnamon

3/4 cup brown sugar

1/2 cup flour

1 cup milk

Who doesn't like muffins? The fruit and only 3/4 cup of brown sugar makes for a sweet treat that isn't loaded with sugar. Try substituting different dried fruit (blueberries, raisins, apricots) for variation.

Combine all ingredients and put into buttered muffin pan and bake for 35 minutes. Makes 10–12 muffins.

A Lifetime of Working
(And Then Came a Hurricane)

Charles McDonald

When Charles McDonald was "coming up," he never thought he would live this long—and he is only 53 years old. Most of his high school friends are gone now. "They died young, but we were old when we were young, if you understand what I mean. Everybody was doing adult things, we just weren't adults." Charles was talking about their working and having to take care of themselves. Drugs, drinking and everything else came later on. "I wasn't in any hurry. I was raised in the church."

"Everybody was doing adult things, we just weren't adults."

There were nine kids in Charles' family. He and two sisters, who are both teachers, had a different father than the two kids before them and the four after. His stepfather was an abusive man, and his mother was in the hospital a lot—mainly from mental health issues stemming from multiple pregnancies and abuse. The kids were scattered quite a bit of the time, staying with various relatives. "It was rough. Really, really rough."

Charles has worked hard all of his life. "I worked graveyard shift my senior year. School took in around eight, and I was working from eleven at night to seven in the morning. I walked from my job at Pit Grill to Biloxi High School. I did my homework on my break and I told my teachers, 'Look, I work graveyard. I don't mean to be disrespectful, here's the homework.' I had to do what I had to do."

Charles dropped out of high school his senior year and joined the military. "I got two GEDs—one before I joined the military, and when I got back I got another one because the records were lost."

In the military, he was store keeper, material handler, control and accounting specialist. After coming home to Biloxi, he did his last three years in the reserves in Gulfport 305th Field Hospital as a medical aidman.

. . . He never thought he would live this long— and he is only 53 years old.

As far as other work goes, "I can do a lot of things from way back. I did the restaurant thing—cooking, cleaning, all that. I started off washing dishes and on up. I did a lot of things to make it through school."

When Hurricane Katrina hit, Charles was in Biloxi. "But I left and went to Moss Point, and man was it rough. I couldn't come back because everything was torn up. I didn't know nothing. Everybody was in a state of shock. That's the way it was. State of shock. Couldn't do much.

"In the beginning, if you didn't have anything with you or where you were at, you were without. The Red Cross started coming around, the Salvation Army started coming around and there were a couple of pick-up points later on that you could go and get MREs (Meal, Ready-to-Eat), water, and different things you needed.

"It was a bad experience—didn't know who was living or who was dead. As time passed by, it seemed like every week I heard of two or three people I knew who were dead. The ones that survived a couple of months or a year later were just falling—just dying."

Before the hurricane, Charles worked for Signal International in Pascagoula. After Katrina, he was part of a skeleton crew called back "to clean up and try to get things squared away and in order. I worked there until they started laying off, and that's when I returned to Biloxi. I started working with a friend of mine that I've been working with for years. He's got a lot of rental property and we did a lot of stuff from the ground up. It was demo (demolition) at first—the before and after . . . some wonderful things; then he just started buying stuff that was burned and we would go and redo it, fix it up and sell it or rent it. As a matter of fact, I was living in a lot of the houses I worked in."

About Katrina: "It was a bad experience—didn't know who was living or who was dead."

For food, "A lot of times I ate on the job. I'd eat lunch, and sometimes on certain days of the week I would get a draw and could buy stuff I could eat that day."

Charles has a government-issued cell phone ". . . for contact, for work, emergencies, everything. They give me 250 minutes a month." This is how his friend contacts Charles when he has work for him.

In the two years prior to moving into Oregon House, Charles was pretty much ". . . pillar to post. It's just one of those things. I was home-less a lot when I was a kid. When I was in elementary school, I was homeless many times. I would sleep wherever I could. I would find unlocked cars and I would get in and sleep before somebody caught me. But I've seen some good days—it's just the way things were. I know I can make it, but I'm old now."

"I was homeless a lot when I was a kid."

Charles said he was uplifted after Katrina because, "I was doing something to help people and it was helping me. That's how I made it." He was giving back. Things were looking better.

When asked if he ever lived in the woods he said, "No, I would find a shed. I wouldn't do the woods thing. That was dangerous there—the woods are real dangerous. You got people coming through all times at night—you don't have any kind of protection. Now the shed, at least you can get inside and jimmy-rig and lock the door until you're ready to leave. If it rains you're okay."

How did Charles hear about Oregon Place? "When you're out in that part of life you hear a lot of things. There's certain places people go on certain days of the week—maybe the soup line. I never did like the soup line. I mean, I appreciated it, but I always felt real bad when I was going there. I felt out of place. Most of the people on the streets, that's where they went. That was a safe place. She (Crystal Raley) wanted me to go there and meet some people." Yes, Charles McDonald is Crystal's "Charlie."

"I was doing something to help people and it was helping me. That's how I made it."

"Basically that's how I learned about Oregon Place—through her. I don't know when initially she done it, but I know when they called me to come and do the paperwork we had to go together. I know it was cold because we went to the Good Deeds Center, and that was when it was real cold last winter. The people were like migrating all the time and when it gets real cold, when they open up shelters, that's when you really get to see it. You see the people who are helping you and you see the people that are being helped."

What's next for Charles? "Oh man, I got to get better than this. I want to get a job. I would really like to work at the VA (Veteran's Administration) Hospital. I worked there when I got out of the military in a work study program. That's when I was going to school at Jeff Davis [Junior College] and Phillips [Junior] College. That was a good experience. I want to try to be a better man every day. Every day of my life."

Crystal is right about Charlie. He *is* a good guy.

"I want to try to be a better man every day. Every day of my life."

RECIPES BY CHARLES

Charles has been cooking since he was a kid, so it just comes naturally to him. His recipes are evidence that he isn't afraid to try new things.

INGREDIENTS

1 head of lettuce, chopped

$1/2$ purple onion, finely chopped

1 whole tomato, chopped

5 catfish filets

1 boiled egg, sliced

$1/2$ cup chopped peanuts

$1/4$ cup lemon juice mixed with $1/4$ cup fish sauce.

CATFISH SALAD

A well-balanced meal in one bowl.

Grill or bake catfish filets for 30–35 minutes at 350 degrees. Put all salad ingredients in a large bowl. Add fish, broken into pieces. Put sliced eggs on top, drizzle lemon juice/fish sauce over salad (or your favorite salad dressing), and sprinkle with chopped peanuts. Four or five servings.

Baked Celery/ Asparagus Spears

For something really out of the ordinary, try this to impress your guests.

Take 5 celery stalks and put 1 asparagus spear inside each one. Smear cream cheese the whole length of spear. Take remaining 5 celery stalks and put one stalk on top of each one like a sandwich. Wrap with bacon strip. Dip in garlic butter. Bake at 350 degrees for approximately 30 minutes. Serves five as a side dish.

INGREDIENTS

$3/_4$ cup melted garlic butter

10 stalks of celery

5 spears of asparagus

5 strips of bacon

$1/_2$ cup cream cheese

Heavenly Egg Surprise

A heavenly version of deviled eggs.

Boil eggs, cool, cut in half lengthwise and set whites aside. Mix yolks, mayo, relish, cheese crumbles, salt, and pepper until creamy. Put one shrimp in bottom of each half of every egg. Then put a spoonful of yolk mixture in each. Chill and serve. Top with paprika.

INGREDIENTS

1 dozen eggs

24 small salad shrimp

$1/_2$ cup mayonnaise

$1/_8$ cup pickle relish (sweet or dill)

$1/_4$ cup cheese crumbles (cheddar)

Salt/pepper

Paprika

PORK AND BEANS SALAD

Combining egg and crushed tomatoes in this recipe (not to mention the tangy hot sauce—a Mississippi staple) makes pork and beans a lot more interesting.

Combine all ingredients, placing the sliced boiled egg on top. Makes two servings.

INGREDIENTS

1 can pork and beans

1/4 small onion, chopped fine

6 ounces crushed tomatoes

1 boiled egg, sliced

1/2 teaspoon hot sauce

SPINACH CHEESE PIE

Good and good for ya!

Drain spinach, beat eggs, then mix all ingredients in bowl. Put in oiled pie pan. Bake at 350 degrees for 1 hour.

INGREDIENTS

Spinach (1 can)

3 large eggs

6 ounces pimento cheese

1/4 cup milk

Salt and pepper to taste

SPICY BEAN DIP

Warning—could be hot!

Mix into a paste consistency. Serve with tortilla chips.

INGREDIENTS

2 cans red kidney beans, crushed

1 medium jalapeno pepper, finely chopped

1/4 onion, finely chopped

1/2 tablespoon mustard

1/4 cup buttermilk ranch salad dressing

TURKEY, VEGGIES, AND CHEESE

A super soup for several!

Combine all ingredients and place in large pan. Cook covered over medium heat for about 30 minutes, or until potatoes are soft.

INGREDIENTS

6 large potatoes, peeled and diced

1 pound turkey ham, diced

1 12-ounce can sweet peas

1 12-ounce can diced carrots

2 cups Velveeta® cheese, cut into pieces

2 sticks unsalted butter

1 cup of golden churned buttermilk

$1/2$ teaspoon celery salt

1 green onion, chopped fine

FISH GRAVY

For use in the woods or in the kitchen.

Mix first five ingredients together, then add two cups of spaghetti sauce. Cook over open fire or on stove. Salt and pepper to taste. Pour over rice or fish.

Note: You can purchase fish sauce in the Asian section of your grocery store or at an Oriental food store.

INGREDIENTS

$1/4$ tablespoon fish sauce

1 tablespoon flour

1 teaspoon vegetable oil

$1/2$ onion, diced

1 clove garlic, diced

2 cups spaghetti sauce

INGREDIENTS

4 medium to large firm
tomatoes

1 medium purple onion,
chopped fine

1 green onion, chopped fine

1 green or red bell pepper,
chopped

1 12-ounce can pink salmon

2 large boiled eggs, chopped

$3/_4$ cup ranch salad dressing

$1/_4$ cup light Italian
salad dressing

2 ounces lemon juice

STUFFED TOMATOES WITH SALMON

A tasty variation of the chicken or tuna-stuffed tomato, and an excellent way to get more Omega 3.

Slice tomatoes in half, making eight pieces. Remove two-thirds of the core from tomato halves with a teaspoon and set aside. Chop the tomato pulp, combine with other ingredients and mix well. Place in tomato halves. Serve chilled. Makes eight servings.

INGREDIENTS

1 can jack mackerel or salmon

20 Ritz® Crackers or saltines,
crushed

$1/_2$ onion, diced

Dash of salt and pepper

$1/_4$ bell pepper, chopped fine

1 raw egg

SMACKERELS

Make over the campfire or in the kitchen.

Mix above ingredients together. Flatten into patties. Fry in cooking oil or butter on medium flame until brown.

FRIED "PECORN" CAKES

Tired of pancakes? Try this recipe for something different.

Make Jiffy as directed on box, then add pecans and cinnamon. Heat oil in pan then pour 3" pancakes in pan. Turn after brown on bottom, brown reverse side and serve. This recipe is good with honey or fig syrup. Serves three or four.

INGREDIENTS

1 package Jiffy® Cornbread Mix

1 cup chopped pecans

1 teaspoon cinnamon

Cooking oil

BLACKBERRY HONEY BUNS

Make 'em in the kitchen. Mmm-mmm good!

Place honey buns in baking pan. Melt butter and combine with blackberries and condensed milk. Pour mixture over honey buns and place in 200-degree oven for 6–8 minutes. Serves five, or cut in half and serve ten.

INGREDIENTS

5 jumbo honey buns

2 cups fresh blackberries

12-ounce can sweetened condensed milk

1/2 stick of unsalted butter

FIG SYRUP

Makes maple syrup seem just plain boring.

Chop figs, put in saucepan with all other ingredients. Bring to a boil, then simmer on low until syrup thickens. Great over biscuits, toast, and even ham.

INGREDIENTS

10–12 figs

2/3 cup brown sugar

1/2 stick of butter

Dash of cinnamon

BLACKBERRY DUMPLINS

INGREDIENTS

1 cup blackberries

$\frac{1}{2}$ cup sugar

1 can of biscuits

$\frac{1}{4}$ cup milk

Dash of allspice

Confectioner's (powdered) sugar

Canned biscuits take on a new, wonderful life in this recipe.

Put blackberries, sugar, milk, and spice in sauce pan and simmer till thick. Flatten all biscuits. Put a spoon of berry mixture on each, fold over and pinch together (like a dumpling). Fry them in cooking oil until golden brown, then sprinkle with confectioner's sugar. Makes 8–10 Dumplins (depending on the number of biscuits in the can).

JUMPING JIFFY CORNBREAD

INGREDIENTS

1 box Jiffy® Cornbread Mix

1 cup fresh okra, chopped

1 can crushed tomatoes

2 cups small shrimp, chopped

2 tablespoons garlic butter

1 medium egg

1 cup milk

1 teaspoon celery salt

$\frac{1}{2}$ stick unsalted butter, melted

This recipe could be named "Meal in a Muffin." Everything you need for "grab and go" nutrition.

Combine all ingredients and mix well. Pour into muffin pan and follow instructions on box of Jiffy® mix for baking.

FRUIT-O-FLAKES

Got a sweet tooth? This will fill it.
A most unusual way to serve cornflakes!

Combine all ingredients. Serve chilled.

INGREDIENTS

1 15-ounce can fruit cocktail

$1/2$ can sweetened condensed milk

$1/2$ cup whole milk

1 cup sliced strawberries

$1/4$ cup orange juice

$1/4$ cup sugar

2 cups cornflakes

Daddy's Girl

Julie Gee

Julie Gee was a *Daddy's Girl*. Her dad was an independent design engineer and her mother was a stay-at-home mom who was a room mother at Julie's grade school in Fort Worth, Texas. She was an only child of parents who never divorced. She was spoiled and always had money to spend. "I had a really good childhood." And then when she was 18, her father died.

"I didn't know what to do. I started drinking and trying to numb the pain, and it sort of snow-balled from there."

Julie had already married and had a baby boy when her dad passed away. She later had two more sons, but her husband was abusive and sent her to the hospital with a broken jaw, lumps and bruises many times. Her sons witnessed this, but her husband had never abused them until one day when he picked up her nine-year-old middle son and threw him at the wall to get to her. "That was the day that I had him arrested and walked away. It was one thing for me and him to fight—that was mutual—we were grown, but you are not going to mess with my kids."

At this point, she and her boys moved to Mississippi. "I have a cousin in Biloxi who said, 'Oh, come to Mississippi—life's lovely, we'll help you.' When I got here, that's not how it went."

Julie worked at first, but since her youngest son had a bone disease and was on SSI disability, she was able to be a stay-at-home mom and take care of him.

She was an only child of parents who never divorced.

Fast-forward to the year 2005. She was living in Pass Christian with her three sons, and for the first time ever, Julie was purchasing a home. She was in a rent-to-own situation with a friend who was applying her rent payments toward the purchase price of the mobile home. Then Hurricane Katrina hit the Gulf Coast.

"They told us it was coming. We didn't leave until the next day. My church was close by, so we went to the church and stayed [through the storm]. We lived north of the highway, so we didn't get flooded. About three days after the storm the ceiling started falling in from all the debris and the rain, and the sheetrock and the insulation and everything got wet and started coming down.

"There was a lady that lived farther up north and her triple-wide had shifted a little bit, but it wasn't torn up and she took in ten families. We stayed out there almost two months. If it hadn't been for her, I don't know what we would have done. She was a really good person.

"Another lady from the church, Ms. Lillie, had a well and we would go over there and get 55-gallon drums of water. For food and everything else we would go to PODs (Points of Distribution). Menge Avenue Flea Market is right across the highway from our church and they brought all the food that was left over to the church because they had vendors over there. Then everybody got emergency food stamps, so everyone chipped in. For a long time, though, we were dependent on Red Cross and MREs (Meal, Ready-to-Eat). Oh my Lord, we ate so many MREs."

In November of that same year, Julie's mobile home was in a trailer park next door to her best friend, Wendy. "Her trailer caught fire. My boys went in and got her kids out—they were two and three. Her husband got out, but they couldn't get Wendy out." Julie's trailer also burned to the ground.

"The next day the FEMA [Federal Emergency Management Agency] inspector turned up and said, 'Oh, you don't get any money because the fire wasn't hurricane related.' I said, 'If you had been here after the storm, then you would have seen.' We had pictures and we appealed it, but we never got anywhere. I pretty much gave up on it."

It was after this when depression set in. ". . . depression from losing everything, and especially losing Wendy. That devastated me. And, I had

"I had always been a mom. I didn't know who I was without them. I could barely breathe without my kids."

lost the first thing that I had been able to purchase for me and my kids; my boys were growing up; the younger two had gotten into trouble and ended up in the training school—I had always been a mom. I didn't know who I was without them. I could barely breathe without my kids."

Julie rented a place from her cousin. "We didn't have any paperwork, I was just paying rent. I had gotten to where I would cut myself when I got really stressed out and depressed, just to watch the blood. It was silly. It was just crazy. It was depression. When I first started cutting myself it scared me, and I checked myself into the hospital. I was there for a week, and when I got back, my cousin had moved someone else in and had thrown all my things away. There was nothing I could do about it because I didn't have a lease or anything. I didn't have anywhere to go."

Julie was homeless. "My oldest son and I were walking down the railroad track. I was crying. I had no idea what we were going to do, and I ran into a guy I knew. I had worked at the local grocery store, so I knew a bunch of the [homeless] guys. They would come in and get beer and stuff. He asked, 'Julie, what's wrong? Why are you so upset?' I told him that I didn't know where we were going to go or where we were going to sleep. He said, 'Well, let me check with my friend that I camp with and make sure it's okay for you to come out there.' It turned out to be John, a guy that I had known rather well. At that time they were staying under the bridge. He had an extra tent and he showed us how to survive.

"Later, my son and I moved to some woods and had our own campsite. It's not great living around a lot of people, so we would try to get away."

Julie became adept at cooking and living in the woods. "It was just like a long camping trip. We ate great out in the woods. We had a campfire. It was a piece of pipe that was big and round, and it was closed on the bottom. It looked like a piece that had been cut off of something. It was like a pit, and I took that thing to every campsite I had. That was how we kept warm. That was how we cooked. We could set things in the coals, grill the meat—it did everything."

In the summer it was too hot to have a fire, so they ate a lot of canned goods. Julie would build a fire early in the morning for their coffee, then

"I had lost the first thing that I had been able to purchase for me and my kids."

"I wasn't mad. I felt like it was what I deserved. I felt like I had failed."

heat up anything they were going to be eating later and wrap it in tin foil to keep it warm through the day. "I would much rather be homeless in the wintertime."

Julie has someone special in her life—he is a year older than her 44 years. "A good guy this time. His name is Jason. We would see each other at lunch or at the homeless day shelter in Biloxi, and we just got to be friends. We would talk and he always made me laugh. We just started hanging out together and ended up falling in love. We've been together almost two years now. He was homeless due to a medical condition. He has worked his whole life—in construction, for furniture companies, and for a long time was an iron worker. He is a veteran and had some heart trouble. He had open-heart surgery to get a defibrillator and a pacemaker, and now he is fighting for his disability. He can't do the work he has always done because the medication he takes makes him dizzy. A disability judge told him he could possibly be a secretary. He is six foot five, has worked outside all his life and doesn't have the social skills to deal with the public and answer the phone.

"When I first started cutting myself it scared me, and I checked myself into the hospital."

"Jason is amazing. He winterized my tent and we never got cold in the winter. He made a canopy so we didn't get wet when it rained. We had lawn furniture—it was just like a regular home except for no water, no electricity and no walls. When it got real cold we went to the homeless handout for the veterans and got some thick winter clothes. We kept warm by the fire when we were outside, and Jason had wrapped the tent so well with other tarps and stuff that when we went inside, our breath was enough to keep us warm—and we had like four or five sleeping bags."

For entertainment they played a lot of Yahtzee and Spades, listened to the battery radio and read. Julie is a voracious reader.

When asked if she ever had to panhandle, she said, "It never did get that severe for me, thank God! That was like the last bit of pride I had. I just could not go ask people for money. There wasn't anything I [wanted that I] couldn't do without. If there was something I needed, I would go clean someone's house for twenty or twenty-five dollars, but nothing on a regular basis. It just seemed like God would bless me. Someone would come along and ask us if I could help them do something and they would give us a couple of dollars.

"And the homeless community—the other homeless—they would give me the shirt off their back. They were so good to me. As I got to be in some of the programs [for the homeless], I got to be friends with the case managers and the professional end of it. They have done a lot to help me also."

Julie's faith in God is a "huge part" of her life now. "It takes my medication, my therapy, my church and Jesus to keep me straight and on the right path."

How did Julie get from the woods to Oregon Place? "I was walking to the bus stop one day and a man in a white van pulled over and said to me, 'Would you like to have a cup of coffee?' I thought to myself, *What is this black man asking me?* I said, 'No, man, I don't want a ride, I don't want a cup of coffee.' He said, 'No, it's not like that. It's not like that.' He told me it was a homeless outreach called HPRP (Homelessness Prevention and Rapid Re-housing Program). I said, 'Yeah—I've heard of that before.' I'd signed up for public housing, I'd signed up for everything I'd heard of, trying to get some help to get out of the woods and none of it had worked out. I had been on waiting lists for over a year. I said, 'You know what? If this is just another story, I don't want to hear it. But if you could really help me, I'd really be interested.' He said, 'Okay, here's my card. Give me a call.'

"I called and set up an interview with Kim. Jason and I went down to her office, filled out the paperwork, and within two weeks she handed us the keys to move in here."

Julie now has a "permanent address." Without a permanent address a person can't get a driver's license or an ID. "Jason had to go three years without an ID because he didn't have an address. You have to have a light bill or utility bill—something in your name at the address where you stay. If you don't have an ID the police know you're homeless and they harass you. There is a stigma that if you are homeless you are a drug addict, an alcoholic or mentally ill. There are some like that, but that is a very small percentage of the people I've met since I've been homeless."

Getting a job without a permanent address is another problem, not to mention the challenge of not being able to shower on a routine basis. "There were certain hours at the church when you could get cleaned up."

"It was just like a long camping trip. We ate great out in the woods."

Julie quit her senior year of high school when she had half a year left and only had to go half a day. "I got bull-headed. I just thought, *Well, I'm grown now, so I can quit school.* I regret it so much."

The only kind of formal training she has had was Women in Construction. It was paid training, and they rebuilt homes after Hurricane Katrina. "I liked it, but I found out I'm too old to swing a hammer for a living!"

Is Julie angry about being homeless? "No, I wasn't mad. I felt like it was what I deserved. I felt like I had failed. My self-esteem had bottomed out. I was depressed because the younger two had gotten in trouble and I felt like I had failed to protect them. But now I know that it was their decision. They are the ones who made the mistake—and they are the ones who taught me that."

When they left the woods and moved to Oregon Place, Julie and Jason passed their tent, furniture, fireplace—everything they had to some other homeless people who had just gotten into town, thinking that they were going to come to Biloxi and be able to work. "There's just not that much work, so we passed it on—let somebody else get some good out of it."

Since moving to Oregon Place, Julie has gotten her GED and has enrolled in a junior college. She wants to go from there to the university and get a four-year degree.

"I plan to become a licensed social worker and work with the homeless. Looking back, I really feel that the reason God let me go through this is so that I will know what I am talking about when I become a social worker and get to help the homeless. There are so many programs out there and their heart is in the right place, but they are not really doing what needs to be done. They come across as Little Mary Sunshine, and the homeless don't want to hear all that. They need somebody who has been there and done that and knows what it's like when you are cold and you are wet. Some of the ladies where we would go to do our laundry would say, 'Well, I don't know why you think you are going to come in here and do laundry, your clothes are all wet.' Of course they were wet—it had stormed all weekend!"

Julie had a setback in January of 2011. She had planned to begin her

> "Someone would come along and ask us if I could help them do something and they would give us a couple of dollars."

studies at the junior college, but one piece of paper she needed from the IRS delayed that until the summer semester. "I got depressed for a couple of months and really didn't want to do anything, but I am back on track now. I've been going to mental health classes, got some anti-depressants and anxiety medication and got into a really fabulous church. They've helped quite a bit, just being supporting and loving."

The anxiety attacks Julie speaks of have been severe—shaking, sweating, heart pounding, feeling as if she were having a heart attack. "It's just from not knowing what the next day will bring. Even though I'm in housing now and I know I'm safe, there is still the fear that something could go wrong and I would be back out in the woods or on the streets with nowhere to go. When I first got here I was scared that something was still gonna go wrong and they were going to jerk it out from under me because that had happened so many times. You know—everybody promising you stuff that never manifested.

"I can't just blame that on being homeless, because I've had a depressive attitude since I was in high school—I just didn't realize it. It's that feeling that nothing's going right, somebody's out to get me, if something bad can happen it's going to."

Julie is emerging from that dark pit and has adopted a much more positive attitude. "A great deal of that is from going to church and having this place [Oregon Place] that I know I can take a shower, be cleaned up, look decent to go apply for a job or be at school. I told an old caseworker of mine, 'How am I supposed to go to school every day and smell like a campfire?' She gave me the little speech about 'Tyler Perry lived in his car when he was writing the Madea plays, and if he could do it, you can do it.' That stuck with me. I'm intelligent enough. I'm determined enough. My dad used to call it bullheaded. There's no reason that I can't do it now that I'm stable.

"I'm looking for employment now, but not as hard as I will be after I get my school schedule—what days I will be in school and when I will be off. My education is my main focus right now. I see that this is the only way I am going to be self-sufficient and be able to pay bills and take care of myself."

"... the homeless community—the other homeless—they would give me the shirt off their back. They were so good to me."

JULIE'S CAMPSITE RECIPES

Most of the following recipes are easily adaptable to indoor kitchen cooking.

BACON & POTATOES BREAKFAST

INGREDIENTS

Sliced potatoes

Bacon strips

1 chopped onion

Butter

Salt/Pepper

Other needs:

Heavy tinfoil

Bacon lovers, this is another great recipe for a camping trip breakfast.

Layer ingredients in foil. Top with pats of butter. Fold up edges of foil and seal. Cook over hot coals for 20–30 minutes.

ALL-IN-ONE BREAKFAST

INGREDIENTS

3 sausage links

3 eggs

1/2 potato, diced

1/4 cup shredded cheese

3 tablespoons milk

Campfire or kitchen—cooking for two or for a crowd, this recipe makes a great breakfast.

In frying pan, cook sausage and cut into small pieces. Cook potato in sausage drippings. Drain. Beat eggs and milk together and add to potato. When almost cooked, add sausage and cheese. Serves two, but amounts of ingredients can be adjusted to number of servings needed.

FOIL DINNER

The foil is washed and reused for other recipes.
"If it was reasonable, we saved everything we could."
Each packet is an individual serving, so make as many
as needed. Works great for hunting and camping
trips if prepared and baked ahead—just put
the packets in the hot coals and reheat.

Layer ingredients in center of heavy tinfoil; season to taste. Top with pats of butter. Fold and secure tightly. Leave room to expand. Place on coals. Turn and rotate often. Cook 20–30 minutes.

Conventional oven: Bake at 350 degrees for 45–60 minutes.

INGREDIENTS
$1/4$ pound ground beef

1 sliced carrot

1 small, sliced potato

1 small, diced onion

$1/4$ can cream of mushroom soup, undiluted (optional)

Seasonings

Butter

Other needs:

Heavy tinfoil

HAYSTACKS

"It's kind of like Frito pie."

Heat chili on fire. Crush chips and top with chili, onion, lettuce, tomato and cheese.

INGREDIENTS
1 bag of corn chips or tortilla chips

1 can of chili

1 diced onion

Lettuce, chopped

1 tomato, diced

Sour cream if desired

Shredded cheese

GRILLED VIDALIA ONION

This is delicious, even for those who think they don't like onions.

Peel outer layers of a Vidalia onion. On a large piece of foil, stand the onion on end. Cut an "X" pattern $3/4$ through in center. Put a good slab of butter on top and pour Italian dressing over it. Sprinkle with salt and Cajun spice. Wrap with foil and set on grill or fire for 20–30 minutes. Turn often.

INGREDIENTS

1 large Vidalia onion

Butter to taste

Italian dressing

Salt to taste

Cajun spice

CABBAGE SOUP

Wonderful on a cold day.

Boil cabbage until tender. Add veggies and sausage. Season to taste. Cook until sausage is done.

INGREDIENTS

1 head of cabbage, chopped

1 can of carrots

1 can whole white potatoes

1 can of corn

1 package link sausage,
cut in pieces (can use sliced,
loop sausage)

Seasoning of choice

CORNBREAD

If someone is in the woods without baking pans, utensils or all the ingredients for traditional cornbread, improvise—and Julie is the queen of improvising.

Add just enough boiling water to above ingredients to make mush. Fry as "cakes" in skillet.

INGREDIENTS

1 cup cornmeal

Pinch of salt

Pinch of sugar

Cooking oil for frying

HOBO STEW

"We did a lot of stews because you can always get canned goods and USDA beef."

Dump above ingredients in pot and heat over campfire until hot.

INGREDIENTS

1 can USDA pork or beef

1 can whole kernel corn

1 can green beans

1 can diced tomatoes

1 can green peas

1 can kidney beans

TUNA DINNER

"Inexpensive and easy to make on a campfire."

Mix all ingredients together in a pot and heat. Feeds two or more, depending on appetites.

INGREDIENTS

1 box macaroni and cheese, prepared

1 can tuna

1 can cream of mushroom soup

1 can green peas

CHEESY ITALIAN PULL-APART BREAD

Not an original recipe of Julie's, but one of her favorites and too good not to share. Kitchen only.

INGREDIENTS

2 tubes of refrigerated biscuits

$1/2$ cup spaghetti sauce

6 string cheese sticks,
cut into 1-inch pieces

2 tablespoons melted butter

2 tablespoons Italian seasoning

2 tablespoons parmesan cheese

Garlic powder to taste

Preheat oven to 450 degrees. Lightly grease an 8-inch cake pan. Flatten each biscuit into a 4-inch circle. Spoon 1 teaspoon of spaghetti sauce into center of each biscuit. Place string cheese piece on the sauce. Fold the dough in half and pinch the seams together tightly to seal in the cheese. Place folded biscuits in prepared cake pan, starting at outside edge of cake pan and moving toward center. Brush the tops of biscuits with the melted butter and sprinkle with Italian seasoning, parmesan cheese and garlic powder. Bake approximately 15 minutes, until golden brown. Makes a panful!

APPLE CRISP

Can't you just smell the aroma?

INGREDIENTS

4 apples, peeled and sliced

$3/4$ cup of butter

$3/4$ cup of dark brown sugar

$1 1/4$ cup of flour

$1/2$ cup of quick oats

1 tablespoon cinnamon

Fill Dutch oven halfway with apples. Combine butter, dark brown sugar, flour, oats, and cinnamon. Cut butter into mixture. Spread mixture over apples. Cover and cook in coals for 45 minutes, or until apples are soft. (Conventional oven: bake at 375 degrees for 30 minutes) Approximately four servings.

PEACH COBBLER

Clever, resourceful, imaginative,
and a favorite of Julie's.

Drain off syrup, reserving $1/4$ can. Mix drained syrup with Bisquick® until it forms a batter-like consistency. Pour batter back into can over peaches. Place any kind of lid over can. Set can into hot coals. Cook until Bisquick® has formed hard dumplings.

INGREDIENTS

Large can of sliced peaches in heavy syrup

Bisquick® (enough to make a batter-like consistency)

PEANUT BUTTER COOKIES

Julie submitted this recipe of Jason's. "I'm telling you, I have probably gained thirty pounds since we moved inside. . . . These are made in a kitchen—food pantries love to give out peanut butter and they give it out every visit. This is a good way to use it up."

Preheat oven to 375 degrees. Grease two cookie sheets. Whisk together the flour and baking soda. Beat in large bowl till well blended the butter, sugar, brown sugar, peanut butter, and vanilla. Stir in the flour mixture until blended. Shape into balls and arrange two inches apart. Press flat with a fork. Bake one sheet at a time for 10–12 minutes. Makes about 2 dozen cookies.

INGREDIENTS

Whisk together:

$1^1/_2$ cup all purpose flour

$1/_2$ teaspoon baking soda

Beat in large bowl till well blended:

$1/_3$ cup butter, softened

$1/_2$ cup sugar

$1/_2$ cup packed brown sugar

$1/_2$ cup peanut butter

$1/_2$ teaspoon vanilla

FRIED CAMP PIES

Biscuits and ready-made pie filling make this recipe as easy as . . . well, pie!

INGREDIENTS

1 can any flavor fruit pie filling

1 can Grands!® biscuits

Margarine

Cinnamon sugar

Pat each biscuit flat. Place large spoon of filling in center of dough. Fold over and crimp edges. Fry in margarine over low to medium-heat fire until done. Sprinkle with cinnamon sugar.

MOCK TOASTED ANGEL CAKE

Mouth-watering goodness!

INGREDIENTS

Day-old unsliced loaf cake

Sweetened, condensed milk

Shredded coconut

Cut unsliced loaf cake into 2" squares. Dip into sweetened, condensed milk, then into shredded coconut. Place bread squares on stick and toast over fire. Number of servings will vary according to how far the ingredients will stretch.

The Slippery Slope of Circumstances

John Morgan

John Morgan, his friends call him J, was in Colorado Springs taking care of his disabled aunt when Hurricane Katrina hit the Gulf Coast. He returned to his home in Pass Christian to help his mother, sisters and grandparents when it was safe to get to their homes. "You just couldn't get down there because of the debris. The military was down in that area. I lost my childhood home and my grandparents' home that was left to me. I have lived out here in Gulfport with family and friends, helping them repair the storm damage. A lot of times we were just trying to make it, because when you gut a house you are pretty much living in a tent in the woods, in the yard, or waiting to get a FEMA trailer."

Tragically, John's cousin was trapped in the attic of his grandparents' home during the storm and drowned. He was 48 years old.

"A lot of homes down here are inherited. The people were just paying their bills, taking care of their kids and paying daycare. They didn't have homeowner's insurance . . . they didn't have flood insurance . . . they didn't have hurricane insurance in order to come back and rebuild. All of these people were relying on SBA grants and stuff like that.

"My mother had three feet of water in her condo. She had to use most of her savings, almost forty-six thousand dollars, to buy the flooring, sheetrock, doors, appliances, washer and dryer, toilets, refrigerator, air conditioning units . . . and there were a lot of pictures and sentimental stuff that she couldn't replace.

"It wasn't like this was a planned move. This was all of a sudden . . . bam! You have to do what you have to do."

"Every man that I know would like to at least have something stable for his kids."

"What she encountered was that if you use your savings because you want to go ahead and get back in your unit as quickly as possible and get it up and running, the insurance company drags it out." Three years later, the insurance company settled for pennies on the dollar—$20,000.

Since that time, John's mother has had to have back surgery. For almost a year, 2006 to 2007, she was at home in bed, unable to get up and down the stairs, so John took care of her. "She wound up moving into an assisted living home in Orange Grove."

Through a series of circumstances and misunderstandings, John found himself homeless. "I was working, but anybody that knows about working knows it takes a while to save up a nest egg. It takes three to four thousand in cash to move into a place. I was in the process of saving money, but I had to find a place to stay immediately. It wasn't like this was a planned move. This was all of a sudden . . . bam! You have to do what you have to do. So I went to stay with a friend here, paying a little rent, buying groceries, and my money was thinning out."

What were John's thoughts and feelings about being homeless? "I was unsettled about a lot of it because I didn't know how my family was going to feel. I had always been out on my own. If I needed to pitch a tent or needed to sleep under a bridge, I could do it and make it happen. I worked in restaurants so eating was never a problem. I had money coming in. My main concern was my family. Every man that I know would like to at least have something stable for his kids. Most guys have a family . . . they want to leave them with a nest egg or leave them college money or whatever. I always had the idea that I would leave my kids and my family enough money to make it hard to cry at the funeral, so to speak. I guess I had a big goal set for myself, but everything is obtainable because of God and prayer. Everything is possible. It is His will."

"I think my hindrance in life was that I was pursuing my dreams and I wasn't going after my gift that God gave me—and food preparation is it."

John is 41, divorced and has two children, a boy 21 and a girl 19. In 1993, the year he lost his father, his 21-day-old baby son died following heart valve surgery. "That was basically the beginning of the end of the marriage—she was hurting about the baby, I was hurting about my father and the baby . . . I could not nurture her in her depression and she couldn't nurture me in my depression."

When asked if he had any dreams for his future he said, "I think my hindrance in life was that I was pursuing my dreams and I wasn't going after my gift that God gave me—and food preparation is it.

"I am a stickler. I don't like anybody dipping in my pots. I don't like anybody tasting my food before I cook it or before I put it on the plate and say it's time to eat. The cleanliness . . . everything has to be sterile. I have a big phobia about people going in my refrigerator without washing their hands. That is the main thing of any food preparation area—the cleanliness, even down to the bleach in the water and the rags . . . it just has to be clean. A clean work area is a safe work area.

"And people who are just now starting off cooking, most of the time they want to pick up a knife to open up a bag or plastic or something. No! Get some scissors. You will save yourself a lot of time and confusion. You use knives for cutting, chopping, and prep; you use scissors for opening packages. It's just one of the rules that I have developed over the years and I always lived by that principle in any kitchen I work in. Any newcomer, anybody that doesn't know their way around the kitchen, give them some scissors. Don't give them a knife."

Obviously not only is cooking John's gift, but it is his passion as well. He has worked at many different jobs in his life, but his experience in the food industry is impressive. It has run the gamut from fast food to the Gulfport Yacht Club.

"Students from a culinary learning center would come to us for practical training. We may have a banquet room upstairs, a buffet on our bar floor and then downstairs there may be a regatta . . . be it a Hawaiian theme or whatever. Since it was a yacht club, there were unlimited expense accounts, so the budget was wide open. They could want anything: It could be bruschetta with eggs with lemon grass, it could be hors d'oeuvres, it could be bacon-wrapped oysters, scallops, salmon or mahi mahi. I cooked a lot of different food. After nine months I became the night manager. I would close the place down and make sure it was clean. It was the fundamentals of working in the food industry for so long that I knew what was expected. It was almost second nature to me. It wasn't a thing where I had to be trained. I saw two executive chefs come and go. I knew I wasn't a chef, but I was a number three cook and I could do just about everything."

> "A clean work area is a safe work area."

> "I knew I wasn't a chef, but I was a number three cook and I could do just about everything."

> "I have some stability to go out into the world."

John is now living at Oregon Place. "I have some stability to go out into the world. The main thing is that I have learned budgeting in the financial class. I didn't learn the value of money when I was growing up—my parents didn't share financial problems. We have nutrition classes, stress classes, and a number of things they are helping us with that I am finding most fulfilling. I don't have any regrets about attending this program at all.

"I am very enthusiastic about the recipes. I wasn't sure how this was going to go, but I was interested in seeing the success of this book. I have been telling a few people about it and promoting it not just for myself, but because of what it stands for. Oregon Place was a gift from God to me. I always will be appreciative of it. I will do anything I can to help."

"Oregon Place was a gift from God to me."

SOME OF J'S RECIPES

Most of these recipes can be used at a campsite or made in a kitchen.

INGREDIENTS

3 pounds ground beef

3 eggs, beaten

1 tablespoon pepper

$1/2$ tablespoon salt

1 onion, chopped

1 tablespoon minced garlic

$1^1/_2$ cans mushrooms, drained

$1/2$ can breadcrumbs

$1/2$ green pepper, diced

MEATLOAF

Got a limited budget and a crowd coming over? This recipe is for the kitchen.

Mix all ingredients in bowl. Roll into loaf shape. Spray pan with Pam® and cook for one hour at about 350 degrees. Let cool slightly and serve. Makes eight to ten servings.

ROASTED CATFISH

This mild-flavored fish is sure to become a favorite—even of those who don't care for fish.

Salt and pepper catfish lightly. Grill or bake in 350-degree oven for 30–35 minutes.

INGREDIENTS

10 pieces of 5 to 6-ounce catfish filets

Black pepper

Salt

BACON BURGERS

Something as simple as wrapping these burgers in bacon makes the ordinary extraordinary!

Combine ground beef with raw egg, salt and pepper. Pat out ten 3-ounce patties. Wrap each one with a strip of bacon and pin with a toothpick. Grill on each side until well done. Makes ten burgers.

INGREDIENTS

2 pounds ground beef

1 egg, beaten

Salt and pepper

10 strips of bacon

HOT WINGS

Great for any get-together.

Deep-fry wings until golden brown. Roll wings in sauce of choice.

INGREDIENTS

3 pounds chicken wings

1$\frac{1}{2}$ quarts of oil

TOAST, EGG, AND CHEESE

So simple, yet packed with protein and convenient to eat.

Make four sandwiches of toast, eggs, and cheese.

INGREDIENTS

8 slices of toast

4 fried or poached eggs

4 slices of cheese

ONE-POT CHICKEN

Food storage is always a problem in the woods, so this recipe for mostly canned goods is ideal.

Cook for 1–1$^{1}/_{2}$ hours, depending on the fire—boil 'til it thickens. Serves three or four.

INGREDIENTS

1 can cream of mushroom soup

1 can cream of celery soup

2 cans chicken (drained)

1 cup rice

2 cups water

POOR MAN MAC & CHEESE

Cheese is a staple at food pantries and provides much-needed protein.

Boil noodles and drain. Add cheese and stir. Enough for two or four people, depending on whether it is the main course or a side dish.

INGREDIENTS

4 packages of ramen noodles

Cheese (any kind will do)

RED BEANS AND RICE

If you've never tasted red beans and rice, you're in for a treat—especially with the added zest of the special seasoning in this recipe.

Simmer all but rice on medium low until thickened to desired consistency. Serve over cooked rice. Makes approximately four servings.

INGREDIENTS

1 pound of red kidney beans (pre-cooked dried beans or canned)

1 packet of Zatarain's® Red Bean Seasoning

1 pound of smoked sausage, sliced

Cooked rice

HOT PORK AND CRACKERS

Cans of USDA meat are usually available at food pantries. This is a good way to liven it up and get a serving of protein as well.

Mix together and let simmer for 45 minutes to an hour. Serve with any kind of cracker. Serves two or more.

INGREDIENTS

1 can USDA pork, drained

10 packets of ketchup from food bar (or 10 tablespoons)

10 packets of apple jelly from food bar (or 10 tablespoons)

8 tablespoons of hot sauce (from grocery store or Popeye's)

6 packets of sugar from food bar (or 6 teaspoons)

ROAST BEEF PO-BOYS

These Po-Boys can also be served open-face with a fork if too messy, but they will be just as good!

Slice bread in half, length-wise, then into 6- to12-inch lengths. Place sliced beef and gravy on French bread. Add lettuce, tomato, mayonnaise and cheese. Serve hot. Number of servings depends on length of bread loaf.

INGREDIENTS

Pre-cooked roast beef, sliced

2 packages brown gravy mix, cooked according to package directions

1 loaf French bread

Sliced tomatoes

Sliced cheese of choice

Lettuce leaves

Mayonnaise (optional)

SPAGHETTI AND MEATBALLS

You can't go wrong with spaghetti and meatballs. This recipe is for the kitchen.

Combine meat and pat into $1^1/_2$-inch balls. Brown for 30 minutes on low. Combine all ingredients except spaghetti and pour over meatballs. Simmer for one hour on low. Serve over spaghetti noodles.

INGREDIENTS

1 pound ground beef

1 pound pork sausage

2 15-ounce cans tomato sauce

1 12-ounce can of tomato paste

3 cups water

1 can sliced mushrooms

1 16-ounce package spaghetti noodles, boiled according to package directions

SALMON CAKES

Salmon cakes are a favorite of salmon lovers everywhere.

Mix together and pan-fry in oil—twelve minutes on each side. Number of servings depends on size of patties.

INGREDIENTS

2 cans pink salmon

3 eggs

1/2 onion, chopped

2 sleeves saltine crackers, crushed

BOLOGNA AND EGGS SCRAMBLE

Out of bacon or sausage? Got bologna? Try this easy recipe.

Cut bologna in small squares. Fry in pan till brown. Stir in eggs and cook until eggs are done

INGREDIENTS

*Bologna

*Eggs

*Amount depends on number of servings needed

TUNA SURPRISE

Not your mother's tuna fish sandwiches! Tartar sauce definitely gives this old standby a boost.

Mix first 3 ingredients, then add mayonnaise packets (or tablespoons of mayonnaise) to desired consistency. Spread on crackers or make a sandwich.

INGREDIENTS

2 cans tuna fish

1/3 cup tartar sauce

Pickle relish to taste

Mayonnaise

SPICED BEEF

A spicy variation of Sloppy Joes.

Combine ingredients in one pot. Place over fire, stirring occasionally until meat is browned. Drain off grease and serve on hamburger buns or crackers.

INGREDIENTS

1 pound of ground beef

1 packet of taco seasoning mix

CABBAGE PATCH

A great side dish to complement any meat.
This recipe is for the kitchen.

Steam cut cabbage for 10–15 minutes. Add onions to cabbage and sauté in butter. Salt and pepper to taste. Serves four to six.

INGREDIENTS

2 large heads of cabbage, diced into 2 inch squares

$1/_2$ onion, chopped

Butter

Salt and pepper

TOP DOGS' DOGS

When out of buns, or just plain tired of hot dogs, try this for something different.

Boil the noodles on fire or stove and drain. Add diced dogs. Serves four.

INGREDIENTS

1 package wieners, diced

2 packages ramen noodles

CLASSIC HAMBURGERS

Sometimes the simple pleasures in life are best.

Mix ground beef with egg. Add salt and pepper to taste. Make into 4-inch patties and grill. Should make about 8–10 burgers.

INGREDIENTS

2 pounds ground chuck

1 egg

Salt and pepper

HAM ON PINEAPPLE

Or pineapple on ham. Whichever way you stack them, they will be delicious.

Mix ham with mayonnaise and mustard. Shape into four patties. Place on pineapple slices and serve cold. Serves two or four.

INGREDIENTS

1 cup chopped, cooked ham

1 teaspoon mustard

2 teaspoons mayonnaise

4 pineapple slices

CRAWFISH TAIL AND DIP

An authentic Southern dish.

Roll crawfish tails in cornmeal. Deep-fry in vegetable oil until floating. Serve with tartar sauce, cocktail sauce, or ketchup.

INGREDIENTS

2 pounds crawfish tails

Cornmeal

Vegetable oil

INGREDIENTS

3 potatoes, peeled, boiled
and diced

10 boiled eggs, peeled and chopped

Green onions, thinly sliced
(amount to taste)

3 tablespoons mustard

4 tablespoons mayonnaise

$1/2$ cup celery, diced

$1/2$ cup dill pickle relish

Pepper to taste

MOM'S POTATO SALAD

A summertime favorite.

Toss all of the ingredients lightly, serve chilled. Serves four.

INGREDIENTS

3 dozen fresh oysters

3 packages bacon

$1/2$ pound cornmeal,
seasoning of choice

BACON-WRAPPED OYSTERS

*From working in restaurants,
John is used to cooking for crowds—
this recipe can be easily altered.*

Wrap each oyster with a half slice of bacon and pin with a toothpick. Coat in seasoned cornmeal and deep-fry for $3^{1}/_{2}$ to 4 minutes. Serve hot with cocktail sauce.

STEAMED OYSTERS ON THE HALF-SHELL

Livin' large on the Gulf!

Put oysters on the grill and cook until they open by themselves. Serve with cocktail sauce or hot sauce.

INGREDIENTS

3 dozen unopened oysters, fresh

Salt and Pepper

CATFISH PO-BOY

*Deep fried catfish is delicious,
but to eat it on a hoagie?—even better!*

Dredge filets in cornmeal. Deep-fry until golden brown, and drain. Dress with mayonnaise, lettuce and tomato. Serve hot. Six servings, depending on size of catfish filets.

INGREDIENTS

6 farm raised catfish filets

Corn meal

Hoagie bun or French bread

Lettuce leaves

Tomatoes, sliced

Mayonnaise

CRABBY CAKES

*You sure won't feel "crabby" when you
taste test this recipe.*

Mix first five ingredients together. Pat out twelve 3-inch patties. Coat lightly in flour. Fry in hot oil until golden brown. Makes twelve patties.

INGREDIENTS

2 pounds blue crab meat

2 boiled eggs, peeled and chopped

$1/2$ cup onions, chopped

$1/2$ cup bread crumbs

2 tablespoons mayonnaise, folded in lightly

Flour

Vegetable oil

INGREDIENTS

1 pound large lima beans

1 pound cubed ham

1 cup chopped onion

2 quarts water

Garlic powder to taste

Onion powder to taste

Salt and pepper to taste

Cooked white rice (if desired)

BUTTER BEANS

Comfort food at its best!

Boil for one hour over medium heat. Lower heat and cook for three hours over medium-low heat, stirring occasionally. Serve over white rice or by the bowlful.

A Matter of Surviving

Howard Brown

If Howard Brown were to have a nickname, it would probably be "Mr. Neat"—or perhaps "The Philosopher." He epitomizes both. He is 53 years old and has seen a lot, experienced a lot, learned a lot.

Howard was born in Queens, New York, and graduated from Jamaica High School in Queens. He was into tennis, handball and basketball—in fact he still shoots hoops. He has spent half his adult life in New York and the other half in the south—Alabama, Florida, and Mississippi. But in Howard's words, "There's just something about the south. I love the hospitality. The people are friendlier, they're more open-minded, and they welcome you here. New York is a fast life, and I never was a fast-paced person."

Life for Howard was pretty stable at first—his dad had a military background and was also a certified mechanic who owned his own shop. His mother was a stay-at-home mom who started Howard on his lifelong love for cooking. However, as he and his brother got older, they realized things weren't so stable between his parents. His dad was a partyer and eventually left home. Howard's grandparents stepped in to raise him and his brother.

"My granddaddy was a deacon in the church, so I came up in the church. We really didn't have a whole lot, so we really struggled."

Struggle was compounded by tragedy when Howard's mother was murdered. "When she and my dad separated, this guy left a woman and

Struggle was compounded by tragedy when Howard's mother was murdered.

twelve or thirteen children to be with my momma. Me and my brother never liked the guy, but we couldn't convince my mom—she was lonely. He was a really abusive man. Actually, he was abusive to me and my brother. When she realized this guy wasn't for her, she tried to break away and he killed her.

"Two years later they found him and brought him back. When they took him to court and sentenced him, he still didn't get what we thought was justice. We didn't get any justice. He got two years for first-degree murder, and he had stabbed her several times in cold blood—left her laying on the floor at her job, in front of the coworkers.

"But you have to forgive, you know what I mean? I just turned it over to God, because at that time when he killed my mother we were, we wanted to do to him . . . whatever."

Within a three-year period, Howard lost his mother, his father and both grandparents. "I've been wounded, but they were all working people—and they instilled in me some good things—I love to work; and as far as taking care of myself, I'm a single guy but I can cook and clean just as good as any woman." Howard's housekeeping skills in his apartment at Oregon Place are legendary.

When Howard lost his family, he started to drink. "I didn't have nowhere to turn, so I turned to the alcohol to try to escape—to forget. For a while it was taking a toll on me. I still drink beer, but I'm in control of it now. I don't have to have it in the morning, I don't smell like alcohol going to work and all that. I don't know how I could do that. I don't have to drink it every day—can't afford it for one thing."

"It doesn't take a lot of excitement to make it through the day for me."

Howard is a laid-back kind of guy. "When I was in school I always caught on quick and never really was a problem like some kids are. I was interested. Whenever they did the functions—you know, on Halloween and stuff like that, I'd stay home and do a model or something. I didn't care for that kind of thing. It doesn't take a lot of excitement to make it through the day for me."

Although Howard's work history is varied, the recurring theme is food. "Pick any restaurant—I worked in it." Howard also worked in the kitchen at Holman Prison in Alabama as a steward. "I would train the inmates—show them how to cook, make sure they had everything. I can still cook on a very large scale." Howard can bake 1,500 cookies at a time and has actually made 2,000 biscuits from scratch by himself.

"I like to say I'm a chef by trade because I've carved ice, done buffet meals from scratch, all your sauces, gravies, rolls, anything. You can't take out the utensil that I don't know what it's for. I've even revised some menus for a restaurant."

Howard was living in Pensacola, Florida, during Hurricane Katrina. "Between Ivan and Katrina, I basically lost everything. Once you lose everything, then trying to start over . . . it's not easy, especially at my age. Most companies, corporations, businesses want the younger people, and I'm fifty-three. The past couple of years have not been easy for me. It's not because I don't have skills—when I walk in the door and they look at me and they see some of this gray, I don't qualify. So it's really been a struggle for me—it's still a struggle for me. That's the reason why I was more of a private person, but I find that that also can hurt me— being private. That and pride . . . too much pride."

About being homeless, Howard says, "I was used to being in a position where people depended on me. And now here I am in a position where I have to depend on people. And it hurt me. I have slept in the streets and stuff like that, but I never give up. I get up in the morning, try to freshen up and look like somebody, and act like somebody with pride and then go talk to people and try to find work.

"But it hasn't been easy. I'll tell you—with all of my losses over the years, it's really taken a toll. I found that being a private person was hurting me, so now I'm not afraid to talk about anything. I wouldn't talk about my parents—my mother being killed, my daddy dying of cirrhosis of the liver—those things bring back a lot of memories. And I haven't seen my brother in twenty-something years. I looked for him, but I don't know if he's living or dead.

"I wouldn't talk about those things, and I didn't want people to know I was in the streets, trying to survive. I'm sure if I said, 'Look, I need somewhere to stay" someone would have helped me. Legally I did what I had to do to survive. And then even sleeping in streets is not legal, but you do what you have to do to try to make it . . . out there in the woods and behind buildings—find a place to sleep, to keep warm, to keep dry.

"I was used to being in a position where people depended on me. And now here I am in a position where I have to depend on people."

I slept under a pier table when it was pouring down rain—one of those little wood tables they have on the pier, 'cause I had to do it. I have great respect for people that are in my situation now—homeless. Not that I didn't before, but more so."

While Howard was homeless, he still ate well. He had a little hibachi grill to cook on. "I put some recipes together from being out there that you would not believe you can do. If you're homeless, okay, but you have to eat, and that's very important. If you don't eat, you don't have your health—you don't have your strength to survive out there. That's what being homeless taught me . . . how to survive—how to eat to live."

Howard got food from the food pantries, and he got money from going to people and asking for work. "I'm gonna tell you something I didn't do, and that's panhandling. I don't ask for nothing unless [I work for it]. I would always go to the businesses, outside in front of the store, and ask them to work me. I picked up work like that—ten dollars here, fifteen dollars there."

"That's what being homeless taught me . . . how to survive—how to eat to live."

One morning, just before daybreak, Howard woke up from sleeping on the pier, and there was a man looking out over the water. Howard said good morning to him, the man said good morning to him, and then started to leave. When he got about half way down the pier, he turned around and came back. "He said, 'Let me ask you something. Are you a pretty good carpenter? You think? Wouldn't you say?' I didn't know what he was saying—this guy didn't know me and I didn't know him. I said, 'Yeah, I like to think I am.' And he says, 'Well, what are you doing today? You want some work today?' I said, 'Yeah, I can use some work.'

He said, 'Come on with me today and I'll give you a day's work. We're gonna go to Ocean Springs, and I'll bring you back to the pier.'

"And so I went out there and I worked. I worked good for him." He told Howard what he wanted him to do, and then told him that if anyone asked him anything, he was to tell them that Dan Tinsdale's got him working for him. "And so he just left me on the tennis court. By the time he came back I did all the work he asked me to do and he was real impressed with that. And he told me . . . he cried and said that something told him to go back and talk to me on the pier. He grabbed my hand and shook it and says, 'Look, I feel like the Lord put us together.' At the time that I needed him and he needed me."

Howard relays an incident that displays the trust Dan had in him: "He had these boxes in the garage and here I am this guy he got off the pier, and he don't know what I am or what I do. He left me out there and he took a chance and said, 'I want you to go through all these boxes and I want you to throw everything away that you think ain't no good.' So here I am going through these boxes and I find this big old jar of money. Now he left me there, nobody around and if I wanted . . . I figured it was somebody's tip jar. I put the jar on the table and did all the work. He come back after a while and I says, 'I got rid of all the stuff like you said, and by the way, I found this in one of the boxes you told me to throw all that stuff away. I didn't want to throw this away.' So he says, 'Well, Howard, you just earned yourself an extra twenty bucks.' But the moral of the story is, sometimes you got to take a chance with people, and he took that chance with me. And to this day I love him, respect him and his wife, Anna. He put his trust in me and respected me. Being accepted in my situation is important. It gave me back my self-worth.

"It's something like friendship—you can't buy it or give it away, you have to earn that. And self-worth in a way is sort of the same way—sometimes you gotta earn it back, and you do that by being truthful, respectful, and work, hard work. Sometimes you earn it through other people, outside sources. I used to think it was all on you, but it's not; sometimes you rely on people, which I wouldn't do for a long time. I try to pass that along to my neighbors here when they come to talk to me.

"You have to swallow your pride and you have to open up to people. So now I'm just open and I'm not afraid to lay it on the table, tell you where I come from and what's going on with me. I find that works better—it's working better for me.

"Foremost, I pray a lot. I got a guy that comes over and we have like a prayer service and we discuss the Bible and stuff like that, and that helps. It's positive.

"Like I've said, I'm not there yet, but I can see if I continue this path I'll be all right. I'm not ashamed anymore."

> "He put his trust in me and respected me. . . . It gave me back my self-worth."

> "I'm not ashamed anymore."

HOWARD'S SURVIVAL RECIPES

Although Howard Brown has a varied and impressive cooking career, his advice for surviving while homeless is very simple—"eat to live." The following recipes are not fancy nor do they include specific measurements and detailed instructions. Most of them were developed by Howard while he was homeless, to provide sustenance—to keep a person healthy and strong under adverse living conditions.

MAC & CHEESE CASSEROLE

INGREDIENTS

1 box macaroni and cheese, prepared

ADD EITHER:

Sausage—bulk, loop or links, precooked

1 can beef stew

Canned tuna

Improvisation is the standard when cooking in the woods—use whatever you have available.

Cook in a pot on the grill in the woods. Can feed two or more.

HOPPIN' JOHN IN THE WOODS

INGREDIENTS

Instant rice, cooked

Field Peas, cooked

Field peas (Southern peas or cowpeas) are actually beans that are picked green and dried. Sometimes black-eyed peas are substituted if field peas aren't available.

Combine. (As you can see, Howard is a man of few words. The amounts in this recipe depend on amounts available, so number of servings varies.)

PARMESAN CHICKEN TENDERS

Don't get uptight about amounts. Use enough milk mixed with egg to cover the chicken and enough flour and parmesan mixture to coat the pieces. If you like a lot of parmesan, use a lot.

Mix flour and parmesan cheese. Dip chicken tenders in a mixture of milk and egg, then roll in parmesan cheese and flour. Heat oil in frying pan, add chicken and cook until brown, about 4 minutes per side.

INGREDIENTS

Chicken tenders

Milk

1 egg

Flour

Parmesan cheese, grated

Vegetable oil

BREAKFAST LEFTOVERS CASSEROLE

A tasty way to recycle. Again—nothing, but nothing, is wasted!

Mix any leftover ingredients together. Place in greased casserole dish or baking pan. Cover with cheese and bake at 350 degrees for 20 minutes, or until heated through and cheese is melted.

INGREDIENTS

Grits

Scrambled eggs

Bacon, broken into pieces

Sausage, broken up or sliced

Grated cheese

SOMETHING SWEET IN THE WOODS

The peanut butter adds nutrition to this tasty treat, and peanut butter is plentiful at food pantries.

Cut honey bun in half lengthwise. Spread both halves with peanut butter, and eat. Serves one, unless you want to share.

INGREDIENTS

Honey bun

Peanut Butter

RAMEN NOODLE TRAIL MIX

This is a nutritious snack that's easy to make, store and eat.

Mix ingredients together and eat.

INGREDIENTS

1 package ramen noodles, uncooked

1 small package of peanuts

1 beef stick, cut into small chunks

1 small bag or box of raisins

INSTANT GRANOLA BAR

Amounts will depend on how much is available and how much you want to make.

Combine all ingredients but syrup. Add syrup until mixture is stiff. Spread in a pan, let set and then cut into bars.

INGREDIENTS

Oats, uncooked

Syrup, any kind

Peanuts, crushed

Cookies, crushed—
any kind available

SAUSAGE TACOS

This recipe makes soft tacos,
but crispy taco shells can be used if available.

Combine refried beans and sausage in a pot, heat over the fire and place in tortillas. "Fold and eat."

INGREDIENTS

Flour tortillas

1 can refried beans

Cooked sausage (any kind),
cut in small pieces

FRIED SPARERIBS
AND SAUERKRAUT

Eating in the woods is never dull—
and often delicious!

Deep-fry ribs (about 4–5 minutes), cover with heated sauerkraut, and serve.

INGREDIENTS

Pork spareribs, cut apart
into individual "fingers"

1 can sauerkraut

PORK "U" PINE MEATBALLS

Kids love to eat these "porcupines." (Grown-ups like them too.) This recipe should be made in the kitchen.

Mix meat with rice and form into balls. Bake at 350 degrees until you see rice pop out (45–60 minutes). Cover with brown gravy or pasta sauce and serve. Serves four.

INGREDIENTS

1 pound ground beef

$1/2$ cup raw white rice

Brown gravy or tomato sauce

SARDINE TACOS

A new twist on tacos, for sure. Howard is a master at stretching available ingredients. Keep in mind his advice for surviving in the woods, "eat to live."

Combine sardines, crackers and onion with mayonnaise or mustard. Place in taco shell and eat.

INGREDIENTS

2 cans sardines

1 sleeve saltine crackers, crushed

1 onion, cut up "fine"

Mayonnaise or mustard—enough to hold mixture together

Taco shells

GEORGIA BAKED CHICKEN

Howard's years as a cook make his transition from the woods to the kitchen an easy one. He also proves, as with this recipe, that good cooking doesn't have to be complicated. This recipe is one for the kitchen.

Place chicken in lightly greased baking pan. Cover with peaches, raisins and peach juice and bake at 350 degrees for 30 minutes.

INGREDIENTS

Four boneless chicken breasts

Large can of peaches in heavy syrup

1 cup raisins

The Seven Stages of Joblessness

Courtesy of Vault.com

1. Shock

Even if there are signs of trouble at your company, most people don't expect to be laid off. Rather than listening to your employer's parting words, you find yourself wondering, "Is this happening?" You only snap out of it when they extend their hand to wish you well on your future endeavors.

. . . you find yourself wondering, "Is this happening?"

2. Fear

Your world just crashed and as you pack your things, you mindlessly say goodbye to your friends, trying to be positive.

Your world just crashed . . .

3. Confidence

Your skills and experience are up to date and relevant, so why shouldn't you bounce back? It won't be long before you line up a job offer. The question is: which one will you take? The job search is your fulltime job.

The job search is your fulltime job.

4. Frustration

The phone doesn't ring and the e-mails don't come as quickly as you would have liked. You feel unwanted.

You feel unwanted.

You'll take a pay
cut . . . you'll even
switch careers.

5. Desperation

You start applying for every job that remotely seems like a decent fit. You'll take a pay cut; you'll relocate; you'll even switch careers.

"I'm going to
be unemployed
forever . . ."

6. Rejection

They turned you down. You give up on the job search. "I'm going to be unemployed forever," you think to yourself. You even believe that wallowing in self-pity might work: maybe the universe will feel bad enough that a job will magically fall in your lap.

You need a
haircut and quite
possibly a shower.

7. Acceptance

You stink. Your beard looks disgusting. You need a haircut and quite possibly a shower. It's time to get serious. No one said getting a job would be easy.

Why Oregon Place?

Oregon Place was established to provide transitional workforce housing for homeless people so they can live in a safe and secure place while learning basic skills and/or a trade that can be used to re-enter the work place and regain their place in society.

The use of an apartment complex offers many benefits to the homeless. Residents now have an address—something required on a job application, or to obtain an ID; they can cook in an oven and not over a fire; they can enjoy safe, secure, warm and dry sleeping conditions.

The residents of Oregon Place have moved from the woods and homelessness into dignity and self-respect. Working through case managers from other Non Governmental Originations (NGOs or non-profits) that serve the homeless population, Oregon Place residents are assisted in many social, health, and educational areas. The NGOs that manage the residents currently have federal grant monies for homeless rental and they pay the rent and utilities for the residents.

As the following Rules for Tenants indicate, responsibility is required on the part of the tenants. Oregon Place offers a hand up, not a handout. It is not for those who wish to take advantage of a system. But—it does offer those who have been knocked down by life an opportunity to stand tall.

Oregon Place Apartments

Tenant Rules

ADVERTISEMENTS: Tenant shall not allow any sign, advertisement, or notice to be placed inside or outside the building without the written approval of Management. There will be NO rummage or furniture sales. No signs, stickers or notes will be posted on the apartment entry door or windows.

ALCOHOL AND ILLEGAL DRUGS: Alcoholic beverages and illegal drugs are strictly forbidden on the Apartment property, including each apartment. Tenant agrees to random drug testing as a provision of maintaining a lease.

ANTENNAS/DISHES: Tenant may not install any antennas, including "satellite dishes" or "mini-satellites dishes," upon either the interior or exterior surface of the building without Landlord's written permission.

BACKGROUND CHECKS: All Tenants will be required to pass a background check. No Tenant will be allowed a lease if an outstanding warrant is pending by any legal authority.

CASE MANAGEMENT: Tenant will be assigned an approved Case Manager who shall develop an Individual Development Plan (IDP) for the Tenant. Tenant shall willingly and actively work with the Case Manager in advancing the goals of the IDP.

CHARCOAL AND GAS GRILLS: Charcoal and gas grills are never to be used for any purpose within the apartment or on the patio or balcony of the apartment. Grilling by residents should be confined to the common area specifically provided for such activity by the Landlord. DO NOT PUT HOT BRIQUETTES AND ASHES IN DUMPSTERS. DO NOT DISPOSE OF BRIQUETTES AND ASHES IN THE GRASS, FLOWER BEDS, SHRUBS, OR WOODS.

DATA ON PROGRESS: Tenants will provide and allow personal data as required by HUD in accordance with the provisions of the Long Term Workforce Housing Grant. All requirements of the HUD grant program will be conformed to by the Tenant and Management,

SOLICITATION: No solicitation of any kind is permitted in the building.

FIREARMS: Possession of firearms on the property is NOT allowed under any circumstances.

FIREWORKS: Village, city, or county ordinances strictly forbid the use or storage of fireworks on the premises. This includes, but is not limited to, sparklers, roman candles, bottle rockets, smoke bombs, firecrackers, or any similar devices.

GAMES: Jarts, darts, or baseball is NOT permitted on the property due to the danger. Archery sets, BB guns, and anything that fires a projectile are considered dangerous weapons and ARE NOT ALLOWED.

GASOLINE-POWERED EQUIPMENT: Gasoline, kerosene, solvents, and other flammable liquids are not to be stored within the building or apartments, hallways, or in storage areas. Storage of gasoline-powered equipment is illegal within a multi-family facility.

HOLIDAY DECORATIONS: Live trees, decorations or greenery (wreaths) are a fire hazard and will not be allowed anywhere inside or on the outside of the building. Tenants may put up lights or other holiday decorations in the Lease Premise and/or the public areas with written permission of Case Manager.

INCOME LIMITS: No tenant can have earned income, either cash or check payment, greater than fifty percent (50%) of the Average Medium Income for Gulfport, Mississippi.

JANITORIAL AND EQUIPMENT SUPPLY ROOM: Tenant shall not enter the janitorial and equipment supply room. Tenant shall not use any janitorial supplies contained in the janitorial supply closet for personal use.

KEYS: Each Tenant will receive two (2) front door keys, and one (1) mailbox key. If keys are lost or stolen, there will be a replacement charge to the tenant.

LAUNDRY ROOM: WASHERS AND DRYERS ARE FOR THE USE OF TENANTS ONLY. THE WASHING AND DRYING OF LAUNDRY OF NON-RESIDENTS IS PROHIBITED. Each Tenant is responsible for leaving the Laundry Room in a neat and orderly condition and for following all instructions for washer and dryer use. This includes leaving the inside of the machine clean. Lint should be removed from the dryers with each use for efficiency and fire safety. Lint should be placed in garbage containers. If the containers are full, dispose of it at your apartment. No one is to allow their laundry to remain in the washers or dryer for 30 minutes without being removed to a basket or the folding table, to allow someone else to use the washer and/or dryer. If the machine is not functioning properly, call Coin Appliance at the repair number on the machine. Management will not be liable for any loss, damage, or injury to persons or property from whatever cause as a result of Tenant's use of the laundry units and/or equipment provided by Owner therein.

LOCKS: Tenant shall not install any form of lock on any entrance to the premises in addition to those installed by the Landlord. If the Tenant has a safety concern, then Tenant should provide written notice to Landlord so that Landlord may take appropriate action.

LOITERING: Loitering will not be permitted on the lawns, sidewalks, entries, halls, stairways, or parking areas. Tenants may wait in the lobby or front sidewalk for transportation for no more than 15 minutes. Tenant must be prepared to verify that they have a scheduled trip with a taxi or other handicapped transportation services.

OBSTRUCTIONS: The sidewalks, entries, halls, and stairways will not be blocked or used for any purpose other than entering or exiting the respective units. No recreational equipment or any personal items, including but not limited to bicycles, tricycles, skate boards, roller skates, boxes, or other toys or materials, will be permitted to be placed or kept in the hallways or stairways.

PARKING: Tenants shall request a reserved parking space for one (1) Tenant-owned vehicle by providing a current vehicle registration certificate to Landlord. Any remaining spots will be marked as visitor (or other) parking. Any vehicle parked in the parking lot needs to have current license plates and registration up to date. No repair work is to be done in the parking lot with the exception of repairing flat tires and jumpstarting a battery. Any automobile with any of the following conditions will need to be repaired or removed from the parking lot within 3 days: flat tire(s), broken window(s), not working/running, leaking fluids, or broken light(s).

PORCHES/STAIRWELLS: Porches and stairwells are not to be used for the storage of garbage, aluminum cans, household items, or to dry laundry.

PUBLIC AREAS: Tenants wishing to use public areas of the building or grounds for meeting or group social activities must request and receive permission in writing from Landlord prior to the event.

SMOKING: Smoking is not prohibited in apartments or in public areas of the building including stairwells. You must dispose of butts, ashes, etc., properly.

SPACE HEATERS: Each building is provided with a heating system. Therefore, for safety reasons, ABSOLUTELY NO HEATERS WILL BE ALLOWED. Heating with range tops or ovens is prohibited.

TRAINING: The objective of Oregon Place Apt is to provide Transitional Workforce Housing. Tenants shall be enrolled and participate in job training and other self-improvement skills, as development by the approved Case Management. NO EXCEPTIONS WILL BE GRANTED.

USE OF PREMISES: Tenant shall occupy and use the premises as a private residence and for no other purpose. Tenant shall not carry on any trade, profession, business, school course of instruction, or entertainment on the premises without written permission of the Landlord. Tenant shall maintain the unit in a safe, clean, and sanitary manner.

VENDING MACHINES: If the machine, including but not limited to laundry machines, is not functioning properly, call Service Company at the repair number on the machine. Management will not be liable for any loss, damage, or injury to persons or property from whatever cause as a result of Tenant's use of the vending machines.

Acknowledgments

If not for the efforts and support of the following people and organizations, Oregon Place would not exist.

Funders

Governor Haley Barbour and First Lady Marsha Barbour and the Governor's staff who supported the concept of housing, training, and social services for our tenants. Without this top-down support, this project could not have materialized.

Mississippi Development Authority (MDA), Disaster Recovery Division, provided funds for the purchase and reconstruction of the project. Jon Mabry, Director; Lynn Seals, Division Manager for Workforce Housing; and Project Manager Sara Watson.

Gulf Coast Community Foundation, President Rich Westfall, and their Board of Directors for believing in our concept and funding $250,000 as a matching grant for the MDA funds.

U.S. Department of Housing and Urban Development, the source of funding to MDA for the Transitional Workforce Housing funds to make the project a reality.

Sonny Woodward, Horne Group, served as the project manager for oversight of the MDA grant funds and requirements. Without his support, we would still be lost in the maze of red tape.

Gerald Blessey, "Housing Czar" for Hurricane Recovery, Governor's Office, was the first official to agree that the homeless needed housing and training. With Gerald's support and tireless efforts, we were able to get the project funded and open.

Staff from Oregon Place

Lance Geil—Project manager who devoted a year of his life, his skills, and knowledge of construction to the oversight of the remodeling of Oregon Place.

Don Sally—A very active board member who volunteered to live onsite during the start up of the project to assist with the management procedures and overall success of the operation.

Scott Wilder—The maintenance director who has, without complaint, lived onsite and worked on the construction of the project. He still handles repairs, manages the clientele, and maintains the physical operation of Oregon Place.

Korey Nealous—Worked for Lance in the construction days and helped coordinate the various stages of construction activities.

Rodger Wilder—Board member and attorney with Bach and Bingham Law firm, assisted in the legal matter of purchasing, structuring, and leasing documents. Also past president of the Gulf Coast Community Foundation, he was our advocate in receiving a grant from the Foundation.

Shantrell Nicks—Board member and attorney who as treasurer of the Mississippi Cares International, Inc. provided her energy and time to manage the payments in a timely manner.

Others

Mark Pfeifle for all the public relations and ideas.

Bruce Ratner and Pamela Lipkin, M.D., for their help in funding the Elias Anysch Markee-Ratner activities building at Oregon Place.

Marsha Barbour, First Lady of Mississippi, for her interest in this project, asking relevant questions and being available for phone calls whenever needed.

Cholene Espinoza for getting the Marsha Barbour project off the ground and devoting three years of her life to it. Also for writing the book *Through the Eye of the Storm: A Book Dedicated to Rebuilding What Katrina Washed Away*.

Francesca Minerva, CEO of Changing Lives Press; Shari Johnson, editor of Changing Lives Press; Gary Rosenberg, designer of this book and the guy who makes us look good.

Ellen Ratner, president of Mississippi Cares, for her enthusiasm, never-say-die spirit, financial and moral support, and especially for her love and compassion for the homeless.

Last, but certainly not least, William Richardson for having the vision for Oregon Place, for taking it from idea to reality, and for bringing the rest of us along for the wonderful ride. He has been an inspiration to all of us, including the residents of Oregon Place, who say that he keeps them going.

Map of the 28th Street Woods
by Bobby Kelly

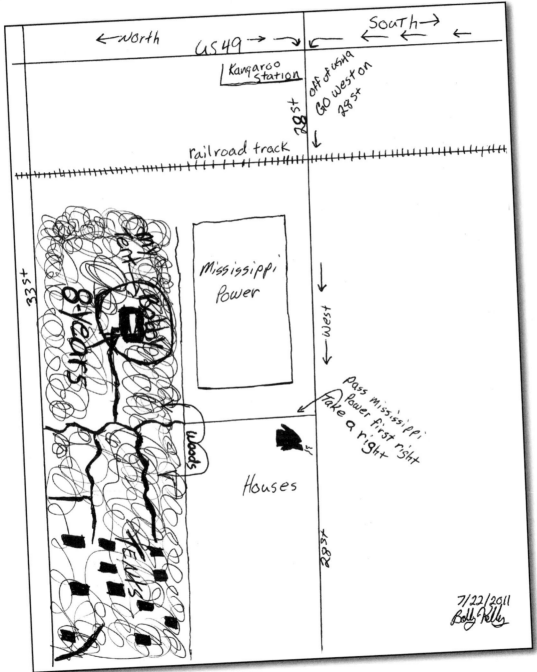

Index